NUCLEAR RISK REDUCTION MEASURES AND RESTRAINT REGIME IN SOUTH ASIA

The Regional Centre for Strategic Studies (RCSS) is an independent, non-profit and non-governmental organization for collaborative research, networking and interaction on strategic and international issues pertaining to South Asia. Set up in 1992, the RCSS is based in Colombo, Sri Lanka.

The RCSS is a South Asian forum for studies, training and multi-track dialogue and deliberation on issues of regional interest. All activities of RCSS are designed with a South Asia focus and are usually participated by experts from all South Asian countries. The Centre is envisaged as a forum for advancing the cause of cooperation, security, conflict resolution, confidence building, peace and development in the countries of the South Asian region.

The RCSS serves its South Asian and international constituency by: (a) networking programmes that promote interaction, communication and exchange between institutions and individuals within and outside the region engaged in South Asian strategic studies; (b) organizing regional workshops and seminars and sponsoring and coordinating collaborative research; and (c) disseminating output of the research through publications which include books, monographs and a quarterly newsletter. The RCSS facilitates scholars and other professionals of South Asia to address, mutually and collectively, problems and issues of topical interest for all countries of the region.

Queries may be addressed to:

Regional Centre for Strategic Studies
2 Elibank Road
Colombo 5
SRI LANKA
Tel: (94-11) 2599734, 599735
Fax: 2599993; e-mail: rcss@sri.lanka.net
RCSS website: http://www.rcss.org

RCSS Policy Studies 25

Nuclear Risk Reduction Measures and Restraint Regime in South Asia

ZAFAR NAWAZ JASPAL

REGIONAL CENTRE FOR STRATEGIC STUDIES
COLOMBO

MANOHAR
2004

Published by
Ajay Kumar Jain for
Manohar Publishers & Distributors
4753/23 Ansari Road, Daryaganj
New Delhi 110 002
and
Regional Centre for Strategic Studies
2 Elibank Road
Colombo 5
SRI LANKA
Tel: (94-11) 2599734-5; Fax: 2599993;
e-mail: rcss@sri.lanka.net
Website: http://www.rcss.org

First published 2004

ISBN 81-7304-569-0

Typeset by
Kohli Print
Delhi 110 051

Printed at
Lordson Publishers Pvt. Ltd.
Delhi 110 007

Contents

Acknowledgements

I would like to thank the Regional Centre for Strategic Studies team for selecting me for the Kodikara Award. This study would not have been possible but for the financial assistance that I received under this award.

I would like to express my gratitude to Professor Rifaat Hussain, and Professor Sridhar Khatri, Executive Director, Mr Sugeeswara Senadhira and Ms Minna Thaheer, all of the Regional Centre for Strategic Studies, for encouraging and assisting me during the course of my research. Thanks are also due to the anonymous reviewer who made many constructive suggestions that have been incorporated in the study.

ZAFAR NAWAZ JASPAL

CHAPTER 1

Introduction

May 1998 marked the dawn of a new era in South Asia. On 11 and 13 May, after a hiatus of almost 24 years, India conducted five nuclear weapon tests beneath the desert sands of Rajasthan. Fifteen days later, on 28 May, Pakistani Prime Minister Nawaz Sharif, claiming he had no choice but to match an adversarial neighbour, ordered Pakistan's own series of tests in the Chagai Hills of Baluchistan and declared that his country, too, had nuclear arms.

Islamabad confidently claimed that 'the strategic balance had been restored in South Asia'. In the aftermath of these tests, both India and Pakistan not only declared that they were Nuclear Weapon States (NWS), but also formally announced their intentions to develop their respective nuclear deterrents. Although both states have refrained so far from assembling nuclear warheads, they have, however, handed over a range of indigenously produced missiles capable of carrying nuclear payloads to their armed forces. Given these circumstances, it will not be erroneous to assert that such posturing by both India and Pakistan would increase the security risks, and make the chances of a nuclear catastrophe in South Asia more likely.

A Nuclear Restraint Regime (NRR) is a central objective in any nuclear environment. However, numerous bilateral efforts, in the form of Confidence Building Measures (CBMs) and Nuclear Risk Reduction Measures (NRRM) have not made any headway in South Asia. Consequently, the longer India and Pakistan remain estranged, the more the distrust that builds up, and the more that both sides can expect the worst from each other. Therefore, it is imperative for India and Pakistan to develop a new mechanism to consolidate and expand the current CBMs and NRRM for a concrete and lasting implementation of an NRR that may help in reducing the security dilemma.

The present work examines the prospects of a Nuclear Risk Reduction Measures and Restraint Regime in South Asia, which would minimize the risks of accidental, unauthorized, or inadvertent use of Indian and Pakistani nuclear weapons in the region. It recommends effective barriers against the danger of loose nukes and facility-related problems. The fundamental objective of this research is to present a scheme that explains the nuclear perils in the South Asian strategic environment, along with possible solutions for viable NRRM and a NRR in South Asia. It may also contribute to the larger concerns of nuclear non-proliferation studies in international politics.

The study provides an overview of South Asian nuclearization that examines the determinants/motivations of the Indian and Pakistani nuclear programmes' development, and assesses their current status and capabilities. The recent nuclear-related developments in international politics, particularly the Bush administration's nuclear posture review released in September 2002 (that calls for developing nuclear plans and capabilities to deter or defend against nuclear, biological, or chemical weapons attacks) have strengthened the arguments of nuclear optimists in India and Pakistan. Recent events in the international nuclear realm are discussed briefly along with the overview of South Asian nuclearization. The various aspects of interstate relations between India and Pakistan are also discussed with particular emphasis on the conflictual issues that exacerbate the security dilemma and nuclear risks in the region. The utility of CBM in the adversarial Indo-Pakistan scenario is discussed with a special focus on nuclear CBMs, since nuclear CBMs between the US and the former Soviet Union laid the foundation of the international nuclear non-proliferation regime, and reduced the danger of nuclear-armed conflict arising from misunderstanding or miscalculation. The current nuclear CBM between India and Pakistan are also discussed in this section along with the nuclear risk preventive measures and components of a restraint regime in South Asia.

The study concludes with the prospects of nuclear risk prevent-ion with a strategy based on the principles of recognition of existing regional and international realities regarding the nuclear weapons proliferation, and building trust between India and Pakistan.

The May 1998 nuclear tests dramatically changed the strategic environment in the subcontinent. Since then, nuclear weapons have occupied centrestage in both the Indian and Pakistani defence and security debates. The centrality of nuclear weapons in strategic discourse has brought a shift in strategic thinking in the region, and led many observers to believe that the India-Pakistan dispute over Kashmir would perforce get frozen, as neither country would risk a confrontation that could escalate to the nuclear level.

This assumption, however, proved erroneous because of India's and Pakistan's belligerent relations. Low-intensity conflicts, limited border wars, and the enormous tension at the Line of Control (LOC) are not deterred by the so-called nuclear balance of terror. Every border skirmish between them now carries the potential—however remote—of catastrophic escalation, and at the LOC, such skirmishes are a daily fact of life. Thus, the dispute over Kashmir could be a tinderbox or flashpoint for a nuclear conflagration.

It has been four years since India and Pakistan fought their fourth war in Kargil in May 1999. Yet, significant nuclear war-avoiding measures and a NRR have not been put in place between them. Many security analysts believe that the Kargil conflict did not escalate into a total war between India and Pakistan mainly because of the threat of nuclear weapons holocaust.

While the threat of use of nuclear weapons might have prevented the escelation of hostilities, it has not brought any significant change in the military postures of India and Pakistan. Both states have continued a military build-up. They have not only tested nuclear-capable short and medium-range missiles, but also handed these over to their armed forces. The surface-to-surface Ghauri-I medium-range and Shaheen-I short-range ballistic missiles were handed over to Pakistan Army's Strategic Force Command for induction on 8 January 2003 and 6 March 2003 respectively.[1] India had already handed over its surface-to-surface Prithvi-I nuclear-capable short-range ballistic missiles to the army in May/June 1997,[2] which placed them at some distance from the Pakistan border. Furthermore, India is expected to deploy Agni-I within a year.[3] These developments are indicative of both sides drifting towards change into the launch-on-warning posture between India and Pakistan.

During 2002, the ten-month-long military stalemate between India and Pakistan testified that the nuclear factor in South Asia could not be transmuted into a factor of stability and maturity.[4] Importantly, achieving stability is a central objective in any nuclear environment. In the aftermath of the terrorist attack on the Indian Parliament in December 2001, many senior members of the Indian ruling coalition, expressing their desire, announced that they were prepared for war with Pakistan. Pakistan announced that it might be forced to use nuclear weapons, if there was a dire threat to its territorial integrity. Hence, in the present scenario, dangerous strategic competition is dominating the security environment of South Asia. The failure of nuclear deterrence between India and Pakistan can have enormous destructive effects for the entire region.

Nuclear optimists in India and Pakistan claim that nuclear weapon capabilities guarantee regional peace, since the fear of nuclear holocaust prevents total war between India and Pakistan.

[1] 'Pakistan N-Power with Assured Delivery System', *The Nation*, 9 Jan. 2003; Qaisar Rana, 'Pakistan Army gets Hatf-V Missiles', *Daily Times*, 9 Jan. 2003; 'Hatf-IV Handed over to Army', *Dawn*, 7 March 2003.

[2] 'Indian-Pakistani Missile Activities Accelerate as Bilateral Talks Continue', *Arms Control Today*, June/July 1997, p. 24.

[3] 'Agni-I ready for Induction into Indian Armed Forces', *Daily Times*, 12 May 2003, http://www.dailytimes.com.pk/default.asp?page = story, 12 May 2003, pp. 4–14.

[4] Nuclear optimists believe that the nuclear factor had been transformed into a factor of stability and maturity in South Asia. They argue that it was the nuclear factor which prevented the Kargil conflict or the ten-month military stalemate of 2002 from escalation into total war.

Admittedly, nuclear weapons have till now prevented total war between India and Pakistan. Nevertheless, they endanger the security of the whole of South Asia. Many security analysts, specially from non-NWS of South Asia, are agreed that the use of nuclear weapons between India and Pakistan in any future war would inevitably result in massive and indiscriminate damage not only to their operators, but also to the entire South Asian region.[5]

Nuclear weapons pose myriad dangers to South Asian peace and prosperity. The real danger, simply put, is that the neighbouring states of India and Pakistan feel vulnerable, since they added the nuclear weapons factor in their strategic doctrines. Professor. A. Sivarajah argued that 'from the standpoint of weather condition and geographical proximity, the direction and effects of radioactive fallout cannot be fully gauged or can be controlled by any means.... There are dangers for the small neighbouring countries, certainly, if anything happened.'[6]

The unresolved Kashmir dispute, deep animosity and distrust, and the continuing confrontation between the Indian and Pakistani forces along the LOC and Siachen Glacier make South Asia a region with a significant risk of nuclear confrontation. Leaders in both India and Pakistan need to acknowledge the dangers and to take unilateral and bilateral initiatives, which diffuse the prevalent hostile scenario and prevent the accidental, unauthorized, and inadvertent use of nuclear weapons.

To encourage trust between the Indians and the Pakistanis, one has to take into account the historical facts and contemporary strategic environment between them. During most of their existence, both neighbours have lived in a state of negative peace—absence of war, but otherwise charged with high tension, distrust,

[5] The author visited Sri Lanka in the first week of Nov. 2002 and interviewed many people, like government officials, faculty members and students of Colombo and Peràdeniya universities, Colombo based think tanks, opinion leaders and informed citizens. They all expressed serious concern about the Indian and Pakistani nuclear weapon programmes. They argued that even if these weapons would not be used in future conflicts, they did undermine the security of the entire region.

[6] The author interviewed Professor A. Sivarajah, Political Science Department, Peradeniya University, Kandy, Sri Lanka on 1 Nov. 2002.

and paranoia. The question now is how can this be changed? The only viable answer is to gradually bring about a psychological transformation. Holding on to hostile loaded rhetoric will not help break down decades of mustrust between the two states.

Political will is an important factor for avoiding a nuclear armageddon in South Asia. To establish mutual self-interest, it is important to deal with the misperceptions and fears about each other. For without resolving this problem, Indian and Pakistani efforts to bring peace in the region will be futile. The process needs action (deeds) and genuine will. What does the adversary want? What are his objectives in pushing the given situation in the conflict? How genuine is his commitment to a policy of conflict reduction and/or nuclear risk reduction at this time? The Indians and Pakistanis would have to seek answers to such questions based on analysis of past experience. The record of the post-colonial era is full of enmity and betrayal. Memories of the past are incompatible with the peace endeavours between India and Pakistan.

Without changing the mindset of the people, regional peace is mere wishful thinking. People can be peasuaded to change their minds only in response to very strong stimuli such as massive transformations versus past behaviour. CBMs could play an important role in this transformation of beliefs although of course, CBMs cannot possibly be a corrective mechanism for all the problems between India and Pakistan. However, if CBMs won't work, nothing else will. They are means to an end, and that end cannot be reached if political and military leaders of belligerent states do not think seriously about building blocks for peace through a process of mutual accommodation and negotiation. Mutual accommodation in the form of bilateral treaties/agreements is a pragmatic move towards avoiding nuclear risks in the region. It is not easy for common people to grasp the realities facing of India and Pakistan but they would follow their leaders if actions spoke louder than words, and would gradually move to support them.

The best way to embark on the road to changing feelings is to complement politically enlightened action by an increasing knowledge and understanding of each other. We have to pursue and sustain dialogue at the level of government, think tanks, and non-governmental institutions like universities and Non-Governmental Organizations (NGOs), so that the deep-rooted mistrust and suspicions which India and Pakistan still have on various issues are addressed. This process will become more authentic and sustainable by ensuring better implementation of the existing nuclear-related CBMs, and negotiating new ones covering both conventional military forces and nuclear weapons.

The immediate concern is how the threat of nuclear catastrophe can be avoided. What is required is a constructive approach for containing nuclear risks in the region. The nuclear risk reduction strategy should be based on the principles of recognition of the existing regional and international realities regarding nuclear weapons proliferation in the current scenario. The nuclear deterrence versus non-proliferation debate does not let the situation improved in the ongoing strategic competition between India and Pakistan. What is the proper approach? In the present regional environment, many analysts think that NRRM and NRR in South Asia between India and Pakistan are practicable solutions to the nuclear flashpoint in the region. The NRRM between India and Pakistan increase openness and transparency in military activities and arms acquisitions, thus helping to predict accurately each other's actions and behaviour. Under the NRRM arrangement, for example, normal military activities would not be mistakenly perceived as being threatening, while military activities that did pose a threat would be immediately identifiable as out of the ordinary, allowing time for an adversary to seek clarification or react militarily, if necessary. Notably, NRRM are not an alien concept for India and Pakistan: both states have already signed some agreements, such as non-attack on each other's nuclear installations.

In February1999, during the Lahore Summit, the scope of NRR was expanded. Both states agreed in the Lahore Declaration to: (1) exchange documents on nuclear doctrines and concepts, (2) give advance notification of satellite missile launches, (3) have a Memorandum of Understanding (MoU) that required both sides to explain nuclear accidents and incidents, (4) improve command and control over their own arsenals, and (5) establish a hotline.[7] The 1999 Kargil crisis, however, undermined the Lahore Declaration, but it didn't nullify the nuclear CBMs in toto, which have been nurtured since 1987.

Nevertheless, the implementation of these nuclear CBMs has been inconsistent, and progress slow. With deadlock in official dialogue, flight testing of nuclear-capable ballistic missiles, a continuing trend towards development of nuclear weapons, eyeball-to-eyeball confrontation at the common border, the existing nuclear CBMs are clearly inadequate. So how can this problem be resolved? The Indo-Pakistan leadership needs to comprehend the seriousness of the threat confronting the two states in terms of the destructive long-term effects of this new generation of weaponry on life and the environment. As the US strategist Bernard Brodie pointed out in the very first years of the nuclear era, the most important task facing the two potential adversaries was to ensure that all circumstances that may lead to a war are avoided.[8]

This necessitates, for example, on going continuous communication between India and Pakistan at the highest levels of the political and military leaderships. Teams of strategists from both states should sit together to understand each other's doctrines, tolerance limits, and the probability of conventional wars. Just as the Helsinki talks between the US and the former USSR became a mutual learning process, such a dialogue will improve mutual understanding and build up confidence, which can prevent miscalculations and misinterpretations. India and Pakistan may join in global efforts to minimize risks through signing of the CTBT and other non-proliferation accords which do not undermine their nuclear deterrence. These issues need an analytical study.

[7] Raja Menon, *A Nuclear Strategy for India*, New Delhi: Sage Publications, 2000, p. 202.

[8] Quoted in K. Subrahmanyam, 'Nuclear Risk Reduction Key Issue for Talks', *Times of India*, 27 July 1998.

CHAPTER 2

Raison d'être for India's and Pakistan's Overt Nuclearization

In August 1999, India made public its nuclear strategy by announcing its draft Nuclear Doctrine. The Indian nuclear doctrine mentions the idea of building a triad of nuclear delivery systems (ground-, air- and sea-based). India has not yet openly deployed a nuclear weapons system: a situation, which in the first few months after the tests, a few strategists would have rushed to predict. In February 2000, Pakistan announced its Nuclear Command Authority. Pakistan has officially stated that it would not be the first to deploy, but would immediately follow Indian deployment. The possibility of nuclear weapons deployment, therefore, is a very real danger and cannot be ruled out in the near future.

Deployment of nuclear-capable ballistic missiles would pose severe security risks given the relatively short distances between major population centres in South Asia and the brief time (3–11 min.) required for missiles to traverse such distances. This factor will compress decision-making cycles for national leaders and battlefield commanders, reducing stability during times of crisis. This fact necessitates that both states adopt certain measures and develop understanding which is essential for non-deployment of nuclear weapons. To chalk out an effecive strategy for NRRM and NRRSA, it is imperative that the motives for nuclearization on the part of both be fully understood.

INDIA

Indian strategic pundits assert that the country developed nuclear weapons because it faces a significant military threat from China and Pakistan, and its security needs necessitate the development of nuclear weapons. They claim that if India did not face such threats, it would have remained non-nuclear. This argument is inadequate to answer the question why India chose May 1998 for its nuclear tests. In fact, India's motivations for overt nuclearization were many and complex. It also poses the question of whether India's national security require overt nuclearization. A closer look at the history of the Indian nuclear programme reveals that there was no consensus among officials in New Delhi about having a nuclear deterrent as a response to the 1964 Chinese nuclear test. If that were the case, a crash weapons programme would have been initiated. There is, however, no evidence that such an emergency programme was started.

Given the relatively advanced state of the Indian nuclear programme at the time, such an effort could have produced a nuclear weapon by the mid-to-late 1960s, relatively soon after the Chinese test, instead of a peaceful nuclear explosion in May 1974, and nuclear weapons tests in May 1998. Homi Bhabha, the then head of the Indian Atomic Energy Commission as well as the founder of the Indian nuclear programme, while commenting on the Chinese nuclear tests in 1964, claimed that India could develop an atomic bomb in 18 months.[1] According to Eric Arnett, 'if the threat [Chinese threat] was as urgent as some observers have suggested, India would have carried out its first nuclear test much sooner than 1974. And India would have actually developed and deployed nuclear weapons and delivery systems, which it has not done.'[2]

The 'proliferation begets proliferation' dictum does not explain the Indian motives behind overt nuclearization. Scott D. Sagan offers a more plausible explanation of the proliferation of nuclear weapons. He argues that:

> The consensus view, focusing on national security considerations as the cause of proliferation is dangerously inadequate because nuclear weapons programmes also serve other, more parochial and less obvious objectives.

[1] Scott D. Sagan, 'Why do States Build Nuclear Weapons? Three Models in Search of a Bomb', *International Security*, vol. 21, no. 3, Winter 1996/7, pp. 54–86.

[2] Eric Arnett, 'What Threat?', *The Bulletin of Atomic Scientists*, Mar./Apr. 1997, pp. 53–4.

Nuclear weapons, like other weapons, are more than tools of national security; they are political objects of considerable importance in domestic debates and internal bureaucratic struggles and can also serve as international normative symbols of modernity and identity.[3]

Prime Minister Vajpayee's decision to carry out the nuclear tests was mainly due to India's domestic politics. Like late Prime Minister Indira Gandhi, he too used the Indian nuclear programme for domestic political gains. Indian political history reveals that domestic political considerations were the primary factor behind late Prime Minister Indira Gandhi's decision to give the green signal for the 1974 nuclear testing. W.P.S. Sidhu argued that 'Despite the dramatic victory against Pakistan in the 1971 war, Mrs Gandhi's party witnessed a drop in its popularity in the 1972 general elections. The nuclear test (1974) was used to bolster its position by representing it as a major achievement for India, which in turn was identified with the ruling Congress party.'[4]

The Bharatiya Janata Party (BJP) was very keen to use nuclear tests to boost its popularity during its brief tenure in 1996. The BJP had apparently intended to conduct nuclear tests, but was prevented from doing so due to its lack of a parliamentary majority, and because of its failure to win a vote of confidence.[5] In 1998, the BJP government started out as a weak coalition that was in danger of losing its hold on power because of internal bickering. Vajpayee was evidently tempted to turn the populist tide in the BJP's favour by conducting nuclear tests. Conducting the tests was the only aspect of the *Hindutva* (or Hindu nationalism) policies, promised by the BJP before elections that could find broad acceptance.

Many Indians who have increasingly gravitated towards the BJP during the 1990s regard the nuclear weapons programme as a

[3] Sagan, op. cit., n. 1 above, pp. 54–86.

[4] W.P.S. Sidhu, 'India's Security and Nuclear Risk-Reduction Measures', in W.P.S. Sidhu, Brian Cloughley, John H. Hawes, and Toresita G. Schaffer, *Nuclear Risk-Reduction Measures in South Asia*, Report no. 26, Washington, D.C.: Henry L. Stimson Center, Nov. 1998, p. 8.

[5] Hilary Synott, *The Causes and Consequences of South Asia's Nuclear Tests*, Adelphi Paper 332, London: Oxford University Press, Dec. 1999, p. 17.

means of gaining more influence for India on the global stage.[6] The nuclear explosions instantly won Prime Minister Vajpayee an increase in popularity internally due to the patrotic feelings unleashed when India became a nuclear power. Praful Bidwai, an Indian analyst, wrote: 'The real impetus for crossing the (nuclear) threshold was domestic, related to the rise of Hindu chauvinist nationalism and the coming to power of the right wing of the BJP-led government in 1998.'[7]

India has long aspired to be in the front rank of global political powers. It has ambitions to play a much wider role than just being confined to South Asia. In 1997, India officially declared that it wished to become a Permanent Member of the UN Security Council.[8] Knowledgeable Indians have candidly admitted that achieving the great power status that they believe could only come with membership in the Nuclear Club, is the raison d'être for the tests. They view the bomb as a currency of self-esteem, and the tests as essential for bolstering India's prestige in the international system.[9] V.R. Raghavan stated: 'Great power status and consolidation of India's claims to it were claimed to be the primary aim of the tests.'[10]

In the Indian Ministry of External Affairs, the view has long been held that nuclear weapons are a key indicator of state power.[11] In addition, the nuclear hawks kept reminding everyone that the US did not recognize communist China until it had become a Nuclear Weapons State (NWS), and that China only became important for the US once it had demonstrated its nuclear devices.

[6] *Strategic Survey 1998/99*, International Institute for Strategic Studies, London: Oxford University Press, May 1999, p. 226; Maj. Gen. Ashok Mehta and Lt. Gen. V.R. Raghavan, 'Strategic and Doctrinal Implications, Post Pokhran and Chagai', IPCS Seminar, 10 July 1998.

[7] Shahid M. Amin, 'Post-Nuclear South Asia—Implications, Challenges and Opportunities', *National Development and Security*, vol. VIII, no. 2, Nov. 1999, pp. 27–47.

[8] Synott, op. cit., n. 5 above, p. 20.

[9] Sumit Ganguly, 'India's Pathway to Pokhran II: The Prospects and Sources of New Delhi's Nuclear Weapons Programme', *International Security*, vol. 23, no. 4, Spring 1999, pp. 148–77.

[10] Lt. Gen. V.R. Raghavan, 'India's Nuclear Balance Sheet', *Hindu*, 7 May 2002.

[11] Synott, op. cit., n. 5 above, p. 21.

They follow the motto: 'Build the Bomb! The bomb means power'.[12]

India's borders with Pakistan and China were/are not secure. Its relations with Pakistan in 1998 had been tense due to many reasons. Sino-Indian relations were improving at that time. The outcome of Sino-Indian rapprochement was not enough for India to ignore China inasmuch as its defence posture was concerned. Therefore, the Indian pro-nuclear lobby insisted that the Indian government develop nuclear weapons to keep India at par with China. They linked issues such as the Sino-Indian war of 1962, China as a NWS, the Sino-Pakistan strategic relationship, and Pakistan's medium-range ballistic missile (Ghauri-I) test on 6 April 1998, to convince the Indian decision makers (in May 1998) that nuclear testing was inevitable for India. Indian Defence Minister George Fernandes used the fear of China for the justification of conducting nuclear tests by India.[13]

India's Nuclear Weapons Potential

The Indian draft Nuclear Doctrine states that the strategic environment, technological imperatives, and the needs of national security will decide the actual size, components, deployment, and employment of its nuclear forces. The recent developments undoubtedly mean that India can deploy reliable fission weapons on a wide range of delivery systems, including ballistic missiles.

Table 1 shows that India has three categories of nuclear weapon designs: a low-yield tactical weapon, full-size fission weapons, and a thermonuclear weapon. Significantly, seismic test analysts have disputed India's claim of the strength of the devices. According to the seismic data, as measured by an international network of seismic detectors, the yields were smaller than India reported.[14]

[12] Pervez Hoodbhoy, *The Nuclear Issues between India and Pakistan: Myths and Realities*, Occasional Paper 18, Washington, D.C.: Henry L. Stimson Center, July 1994, p. 5.

[13] Ganguly, op. cit., n. 9 above, pp. 148–77.

[14] David Albright, 'The Shots Heard Around the World', *The Bulletin of Atomic Scientists*, vol. 54, no. 4, July/Aug. 1998, http://www.thebulletin.org/issues/1998/ja98/ja98albright.html

TABLE 1: INDIA'S NUCLEAR WEAPONS POTENTIAL

Date of tests	Type	Total number of tests	Yield	Possible target/use
18 May 74	Fission	1	15 kilotons	Peaceful nuclear explosion
	Thermonuclear device (fusion)	1	43 kilotons	Strategic application
11 May 98	Fission device	1	12 kilotons	Tactical/strategic missiles and bombers
	Low-yield weapon (fission)	1	200 tons, or less than a kiloton (sub-kiloton)	Tactical application
13 May 98	Low-yield fission	2	Between 0.2 and 0.6 kiloton	Tactical application

Sources: 1. Neil Joeck, 'Nuclear Relations in South Asia', in Joseph Cirincione, ed., *Repairing the Regime: Preventing the Spread of Weapons of Mass Destruction*, New York: Routledge, 2000, p. 134.

2. David Albright, 'The Shots Heard Around the World', *The Bulletin of Atomic Scientists*, vol. 54, no. 4, July/Aug. 1998.

3. http://www.thebulletin.org/issues/1998/ja98/ja98albright.html

According to the Indian official announcement, India also conducted a thermonuclear test in May 1998. Many experts disagree on India's ability to build and successfully test a two-stage thermonuclear device with such a low yield. The experts who believed that India had tested a boosted fission device were surprised by India's statement that it had instead detonated a thermonuclear device. According to Dr R. Chidambaram, Chairman of the Indian Atomic Energy Commission, all that the lone thermonuclear test has done is to enable India to perhaps upscale the design and to produce a 200-kiloton fusion weapon.[15]

[15] Bharat Karnad, 'India's Force Planning Imperative: The Thermonuclear Option', in D.R. Sardesai and Raju G.C. Thomas, eds., *Nuclear India in the Twenty-First Century*, New York: Palgrave-Macmillan, 2002, p. 111.

Nuclear Non-Proliferation: India's Perspective

Since the dawn of the nuclear weapons era, India has been an ardent supporter of nuclear disarmament without embracing its norms. India's first prime minister, Jawaharlal Nehru, made several proposals for nuclear disarmament at the United Nations and other international forums. T.V. Paul claimed that 'India was an active member of the United Nation Disarmament Committee that negotiated nuclear and conventional disarmament before the superpowers began [the] bilateral arms-control process'.[16] The important proposals that India made include the treaty for nuclear testing, and a non-discriminatory Non-Proliferation Treaty (NPT).

In the aftermath of India's defeat in the 1962 Sino-Indian Himalayan border war and China's nuclear test in 1964, India's position on nuclear weapons changed dramatically. Therefore, since the mid-1960s, India's diplomatic opposition to the NPT has been based on its special security needs. When negotiations were underway for the NPT, India attempted to seek a special-case status. It tried to exploit the then prevalent anti-Chinese sentiments to forward its own designs.[17] In 1967, the then External Minister of India, Mr Chagla, while addressing the Eighteen Nations Disarmament Conference, stated:

> NPT should not be a discriminatory or unequal treaty.... India's peculiar position with regard to the NPT is that it is a non-aligned country not in military alliance with any country or under the nuclear umbrella of any country. Secondly, India is far advanced in nuclear research, and third, it is under the continuing threat and menace of China, which has already become a nuclear power.[18]

On 5 April 1968, the then Prime Minister Indira Gandhi stated in the Indian Parliament that India refused to sign the NPT on the basis of:

[16] T.V. Paul, 'India, the International System, and Nuclear Weapons', in Sardesai and Thomas, ibid., p. 91.

[17] Robin Ranger, *Arms and Politics 1958–78, Arms Control in a Changing Political Context*, Canada: Macmillan, 1979, p. 137.

[18] Akhtar Ali, *Pakistan's Nuclear Dilemma: Energy and Security Dimensions*, Karachi: Economic Research Unit, 1984, p. 30.

Enlightened self-interest and considerations of national security.... Nuclear weapon powers insist on their right to continue to manufacture more nuclear weapons. This is a situation that cannot be viewed with equanimity by non-nuclear countries, especially as they are called upon to undertake not to manufacture or acquire nuclear weapons for their defense.[19]

The Indians argue that they oppose the NPT because the main objective of the treaty is *disarming the unarmed, rather than genuine global nuclear disarmament.* This proves that India would give up its nuclear arms only in case of total disarmament. It wants even the NWS (the US, Russia, China, United Kingdom, and France) to give up their nuclear arms.

Though India proposed the so-called 'standstill agreement' on nuclear testing in 1954,[20] it refused to sign the 1996 UN-approved draft of CTBT. India was among the co-sponsor of the talks for a ban on nuclear testing started at the Conference on Disarmament in Geneva in January 1994. The change in the Indian stance came when India linked its signing of the CTBT with a time-bound plan for global disarmament. Pranab Mukherji, the then External Affairs Minister, in his address to the UN General Assembly said: 'In our view, the CTBT must be an integral step in the process of nuclear disarmament.... The CTBT must contain a binding commitment on [the] international community, especially the nuclear weapon states, to take further measures within an agreed time-frame towards the creation of [a] nuclear free world.'[21] India voted against the CTBT, arguing that the treaty was flawed and discriminatory. In addition, India viewed the Entry-Into-Force provision as infringing upon its sovereign right to decide whether it should or should not accede to such a treaty.

India denounced Pakistan's proposals for creating South Asia as a nuclear weapon–free zone and other nuclear arms control–related proposals, because Indian strategic analysts argue that

[19] Paul, op. cit., n. 16 above, p. 92.

[20] Jozef Goldblat, 'The CTBT Negotiations', *UNIDIR Newsletter*, Special Issue, Geneva: UN, July 1997, pp. 5–11.

[21] Bhavani Paul Raj, 'India and the CTBT: From Advocacy to Opposition', in Rouben Azizan, ed., *Nuclear Developments in South Asia and the Future of Global Arms Control*, Wellington: Centre for Strategic Studies, 2001, p. 121.

India's defence needs and security perceptions are not linked to Pakistan alone. At the time of the nuclear weapon tests in May 1998, India argued that it considered China as enemy number one, and it needed the nuclear option to face a possible conflict with China. In announcing its first round of three simultaneous nuclear tests on 11 May 1998, New Delhi set forth its arms control policy. The statement read:

> India remains committed to a speedy process of nuclear disarmament leading to total and global elimination of nuclear weapons. Our adherence to the Chemical Weapons Convention and the Biological Weapons Convention is evidence of our commitment to any global disarmament regime, which is non-discriminatory and verifiable. We shall also be happy to participate in the negotiations for the conclusion of a fissile material cut-off treaty in the Geneva-based Conference on Disarmament.[22]

PAKISTAN

The principal factor which drove Pakistan towards a nuclear arms build-up was the need to provide adequate security for its sovereign existence. Pakistan's security perceptions are largely influenced by the state of its relationship with India. Threats to undo Pakistan have been frequently issued directly or indirectly by the Indian leadership since 1947. In addition, India's own vision for itself in the South Asian region alarms the security of its small neighbours, since coercive diplomacy accompanied by frequent displays of Indian might is an important device of Indian policy to influence its neighbours.

India's annexation of the Portuguese territory of Goa and the independent kingdom of Sikkim, its use of force in the East Pakistan crisis of 1971 and in the Tamil insurgency in Sri Lanka, its intervention in the Maldives in 1988, and its massive use of force in suppressing the ongoing Kashmiri struggle for freedom

[22] Government of India press statement on 11 May 1998 on the nuclear tests, New Delhi: Press Information Bureau, 11 May 1998, pp. 2–3, taken from Brahma Chellaney, 'India's Nuclear Planning, Force Structure, Doctrine and Arms Control Posture', in Digumarti Bhaskara Rao, ed., *Nuclear Materials Issue and Concerns*, vol. 11, New Delhi: Discovery Publishing, 2001, p. 986.

are grim reminders of India's domineering attitude towards its neighbours. The Indira Doctrine of 1983 revealed the Indian design of hegemony in the region. In many ways, this is an Indian version of the Monroe Doctrine. Pakistan on the other hand, seeks equality with India as a sovereign state. The many divergences in the external affairs stances perpetuate antagonism between India and Pakistan.

The end of the Cold War had detrimental consequences for Pakistan. The end of superpower rivalry reduced Pakistan's geo-strategic importance and removed American incentives to continue supporting it. For example, in 1989, after the withdrawal of the former Soviet Union from Afghanistan, Pakistan lost much of its political leverage with the US. This was manifested in the Pressler Amendment suspending the hefty US$4.1 billion arms package to Pakistan and prohibiting future assistance as well as interrupting transactions that had already been concluded, such as the sale of F-16s.[23]

The American cut-off policy vis-à-vis Pakistan damaged Pakistan's access to foreign military equipment. Moreover, Pakistan's weak economy also prevented it from procuring the best available military equipment from suppliers outside the US. As a result, this widened the conventional military gap between India and Pakistan.

Pakistan's insecurity increased multitudinously on 11 May 1998, when India tested its nuclear devices and the then Indian Home Minister L.K. Advani asked Pakistan on 18 May 1998 to realize the change in the geo-strategic environment. He threatened to 'deal firmly' with Pakistan if it did not roll back its proxy war in Kashmir in light of 'the change in the geo-strategic situation in

[23] The Pressler Amendment prohibits US military and economic assistance to Pakistan unless the US president certifies annually that Pakistan does not possess a nuclear explosive device, and that the proposed assistance will significantly reduce the chance it will possess one in future. Passed in 1985, it became a major factor shaping US policy in 1990, when the first Bush administration could no longer certify that Pakistan met the standards set out in the legislation. See *A New US Policy Towards India and Pakistan*, Report of an Independent Task Force, Washington, D.C.: Council on Foreign Relations, 1997, p. 43.

the region'.[24] The international community under the leadership of the US tried to engage Pakistan in diplomatic entreaties for dissuading it from responding with its own nuclear weapon tests. However, before opting for nuclear testing, Pakistan judged its security needs and options at three levels. These were as follows.

1. *Defence by Conventional Weapons.* Pakistan's conventional weapons capability has been deteriorating since the end of the Cold War, and the threat from nuclear weapons cannot be diffused by conventional armaments. Thus, to counter possible Indian aggression, Pakistan would require more than a conventional weapons shield.
2. *Defence by External Protectors.* Pakistan could have sought a nuclear security umbrella against India similar to the one which NATO members enjoy under the nuclear shield of the US, Great Britain and France, or which Japan has had through its security arrangements with the US. The historical experience of Pakistan, however, went against that option. Past experience prompted Pakistan to realize that none of the states envisaged as possible external protectors would either be inclined or able to rush to Islamabad's defence when it needed them most.
3. *Defence by Nuclear Deterrence.* The inadequacy of the aforementioned two options led Pakistan to rely on its own resources, rather than on external protectors for its security. This 'look within' or 'self-help' strategy justified Pakistan's overt acquisition of nuclear weapons capability and their delivery systems. Pakistan, seeking to validate its nuclear weapon designs and buttress the credibility of its deterrent vis-à-vis India tested its nuclear weapons on 28 May 1998. The nuclear tests enhanced Pakistan's national security interests and re-established the strategic balance within the subcontinent.[25] The foreign office

[24] Ashley J. Tellis, *India's Emerging Nuclear Posture: Between Recessed Deterrent and Ready Arsenal*, Washington, D.C.: Rand, 2001, p. 2.

[25] During the Cold War, nuclear weapons played a central role in the US strategic policies towards the former Soviet Union: Gen. Andress J. Goodpaster, *An Evolving US Nuclear Posture*, Washington, D.C.: Henry L. Stimson Center, 1995, p. 6.

of Pakistan stated: 'We are not interested in a nuclear or conventional arms race.... In future, too, we will continue to conduct ourselves with restraint and responsibility.... While we will not provoke escalation, our responses will be calibrated to respond to any provocation or escalation by India.'[26]

Pakistan's Nuclear Weapons Potential

Pakistan had been viewed as a nuclear weapons-capable state, since the mid-1980s, but it was India's nuclear explosions on 11 and 13 May 1998 and its leaders' faulty perceptions regarding Pakistan's nuclear weapons potential that left it with no option but to resort to nuclear weapons testing. Pakistan conducted a total of six nuclear explosions in the Chagai hills in Baluchistan province. It used enriched Uranium (U-235) for those tests.

Table 2 shows that Pakistan has two categories of nuclear weapon designs: a low-yield tactical weapon, and a full-size fission weapon.

The Pakistani scientists who participated in the May 1998 nuclear weapons tests claimed that the six nuclear weapons explosions provided them sufficient data about the nuclear weapons.[27] This data gives them confidence in existing (non-tested) designs and provides useful information for future nuclear weapons manufacturing. Following the tests in May 1998, Pakistan now possesses the capability to develop the following types of nuclear weapons:

1. the non-tested gun-barrel model; and
2. the tested nuclear devices, strategic and tactical.

The international community had questioned the claim of Pakistani scientists about the success of the six tests. According to US Pentagon sources, three of the five devices on 28 May 1998 did not explode. Moreover, the analysis of the seismic data does not support the claims of Pakistani scientists. The average

[26] The quote taken from Nazir Kamal, *Pakistani Perceptions and Prospects of Reducing the Nuclear Danger in South Asia*, Cooperative Monitoring Center Occasional Paper, US: Sandia National Laboratories, Jan. 1999.

[27] 'CTBT Not to Affect N-Programme: Dr Qadeer', *Muslim*, 15 Sep. 1998.

TABLE 2: PAKISTAN'S NUCLEAR WEAPONS POTENTIAL

Date of tests	Type	Total number	Yield	Possible target/use
28 May 1998	Largest explosion (boosted fission)	1	30 kilotons	Strategic application
	Small, low-yield device (fusion)	4	Collective yield of 4=10 kilotons	Tactical application
30 May 1998	Miniaturized version size and weight of the reduced (fission)	1	15–18 kilotons	Tactical/strategic application bombers

Sources: 1. Umer Farooq, 'Pakistan Capable of Building H. Bomb', *Nation* (Islamabad), 1 June 1998; 'Fission Technology has Paved Way for Hydrogen Bomb', *Nation* (Islamabad), 1 June 1998.
2. Anwar Iqbal, 'Pakistan Tested Boosted Fission Devices: Khan', *News* (Islamabad/Rawalpindi), 30 May 1998; 'Pakistan: The Other Shoe Drops', *The Bulletin of Atomic Scientists*, July/Aug. 1998, pp. 24, 25.

magnitude reported by the 65 stations recording the event on 28 May was 4.9, indicating an explosive yield in-between the 6 to 13 kiloton ranges; 51 stations recorded the event on 30 May, with an average magnitude of 4.3, indicating an explosion in the 2 to 8 kiloton ranges.

Pentagon and seismic records also testify that Pakistan faced design and engineering problems in its three tests on 28 May 1998. But they did not deny the reality that Pakistan possessed tested nuclear weapons capability, because Pakistan's nuclear programme is based on centrifugal technology (or enriched Uranium). The enrichment of the Highly Enriched Uranium (HEU) used in the Hiroshima bomb has never been publicly released. However, the enrichment technology used at that time could not enrich Uranium over 80 per cent. According to knowledgeable individuals, the Hiroshima bomb contained roughly 70 per cent enriched Uranium. In fact, according to scientists, HEU (enriched to more than 20 per cent in the U-235 isotope) had been used in the nuclear weapon. Therefore, even if we accept the Pentagon and seismic calculations as accurate, we are forced to accept the credibility of Pakistan's nuclear weapons programme.

Nuclear Non-Proliferation: Pakistan's Perspective

Nuclear arms control has failed to gain a significant domestic constituency in Pakistan. Despite this, the Government of Pakistan has not entirely opposed the Nuclear Non-Proliferation Regime (NNPR). It supports all equitable and multilateral measures to control the spread of nuclear weapons. Practically, Pakistan is not observing the rules and regulations of NNPR. Official Pakistani statements, both immediately after the nuclear tests and later, have advocated restraint on the issue of nuclearization, indicating cognizance of the importance of avoiding a regional nuclear arms competition, both for security and economic reasons. These proposals include a Nuclear Restraint Regime in South Asia, a convention to commit all states to the elimination of nuclear weapons,[28] etc. Nevertheless, Pakistan has ruled out any unilateral decision regarding its nuclear weapons programme—cap, roll back, and finally eliminate. To be precise, Pakistan's policy regarding the NNPR is guided by its security needs.

Many security analysts argued that the regional approach to nuclear non-proliferation and disarmament is complementary to international endeavours towards de-nuclearization. Christoph Bertram argued, 'As the South Asian experience once again demonstrates, however, the main push to go nuclear lies in regional competition and conflict. Global arms restraint will, therefore, only be effective if underpinned by regional arrangements of cooperation.'[29] Gen. K.M. Arif (retd) wrote: 'If South Asia is to be denuclearized, India has to lead the way in a meaningful and verifiable manner. The American advice for a "standstill", as that country's previous demand of "capping, rollback and elimina-

[28] Munir Akram, Ambassador of Pakistan, 'Fissile Material Treaty', statement at the Conference on Disarmament, 11 Aug. 1998.

[29] Christoph Bertram, 'The Future of Deterrence and Non-Proliferation in the Asian Context', in Jasjit Singh, ed., *Asia's New Dawn: The Challenges to Peace and Security*, New Delhi: Knowledge World, 2000, p. 180.

tion" of the nuclear program, is worthy of consideration only if it is simultaneously and equally applied to India and Pakistan.'[30]

Pakistan considers the NPT deficient in several respects, but neither does it reject it outright, nor does it demand global disarmament as a precondition for accepting restrictions on its nuclear programme. Pakistan's security problem vis-à-vis India shapes its attitude, and its leaders are willing to undertake any commitment jointly with India for controlling the possible proliferation of nuclear weapons in South Asia. In June 1968, the then Foreign Minister of Pakistan Mian Arshad Hussain stated that the government's attitude towards the NPT would be determined by whether India retained the option to make nuclear weapons.[31] Subsequently, Pakistan announced that it would never sign the NPT until India did so. This has been a consistent policy of all the Pakistani governments since the 1960s.

Pakistan's interest in constituting South Asia as a Nuclear Weapons Free Zone pre-dates India's May 1974 nuclear explosion.[32] In the Sixth Annual Session of the UN Atomic Energy Conference held in Mexico in September 1972, Pakistan put forward a proposal to denuclearize South Asia. In September 1974, Pakistan first tabled the South Asian Nuclear Weapon Free Zone (NWFZ) proposal in the UN General Assembly. On 5 September 1974, UN Secretary General Kurt Waldheim, in his introduction to his annual report to the forthcoming UN General Assembly Session, extended his support to Pakistan's NWFZ proposal. He stated that 'I consider such initiatives as not only useful but a necessary part of our search for universal disarmament.' The then Indian permanent representative to the UN, Mr Rikhi Jaipal, came out in strong opposition to the Pakistani proposal. Significantly, despite India's opposition, Pakistan has reiterated the NWFZ proposal in every General Assembly session.

[30] The quote was taken from Kamal, op. cit., n. 26 above.

[31] *Dawn*, 1 July 1968.

[32] Samina Ahmad, 'Pakistan's Proposal for a Nuclear Weapon Free Zone in South Asia', *Pakistan Horizon*, vol. XXXII, no. 4, Karachi: 1979, pp. 92–130; also see Ashley J. Tellis, *Stability in South Asia*, Rand Report, Washington D.C.: Arroyocenter, 1997, p. 42.

In addition to NWFZ, Pakistan had made many proposals for curbing nuclear proliferation in the region. In the aftermath of the May nuclear tests, the prospects for NWFZSA ended. Recently, however, once again Pakistan reiterated its earlier NWFZSA. In response to a question during an interview broadcast on 4 May 2003 night on television channel ARY, the president of Pakistan said that if the Kashmir dispute was resolved, there would be peace and security in the region, and 'South Asia could be denuclearised mutually by India and Pakistan.'[33]

Significantly, Pakistan had proposed a wide range of nuclear arms control measures to India before the May 1998 nuclear tests.

1. In 1978, formal renunciation by South Asian states of acquisition and manufacture of nuclear weapons.
2. In 1979, simultaneous adherence to the NPT.
3. In 1979, simultaneous acceptance of full-scope IAEA safeguards for all nuclear installations.
4. In 1979, mutual inspection of each other's nuclear facilities.
5. In 1987, a bilateral or regional nuclear test ban treaty.
6. In 1986, the then Prime Minister of Pakistan Mohammad Khan Junejo reiterated Pakistan's nuclear arms control proposals. He offered to accept binding obligations if India reciprocated.
7. In 1991, the convocation of a five-nation meeting to resolve the problem of nuclearization of South Asia with the participation of India and Pakistan, as well as the US, Russia, and China. According to former US Secretary of State James Baker, India was the only opponent to the proposal for a five-power conference.
8. In 1993, the establishment of a South Asia Zero Missile Zone.
9. In 1996, the Multilateral Conference on Security, Arms Control and Non-Proliferation in South Asia.

Pakistan does not have any problem with the CTBT in principle. Following the May tests, Pakistan has acted with restraint by declaring a unilateral moratorium and offered India a regional test

[33] 'Musharraf Links Nuke-Free S Asia to Kashmir Solution', *Daily Times*, 5 May 2003.

ban treaty. The then Prime Minister Mohammad Nawaz Sharif, in his address to the UN General Assembly on 23 September 1998 had declared Pakistan's readiness to adhere to the CTBT, provided the coercive atmosphere arising from sanctions against it was removed.[34]

On 16 December 1993, the UN General Assembly adopted a resolution which called for the negotiation of 'a non-discriminatory, multilateral and internationally and effectively verifiable treaty banning the production of fissile material for nuclear weapons or other nuclear explosive devices'.[35] On 30 July 1998, the then Pakistani Ambassador to the UN at Geneva, Mr Munir Akram, stated that 'Pakistan has consistently believed that a ban on the production of fissile materials should be promoted through a universal and non-discriminatory treaty in the CD and not through unilateral measures.' He also announced that Pakistan would join in promoting a decision for the establishment of an ad hoc committee to conduct negotiations.[36] But at the same time, Pakistan made it clear that it could not agree to any demand for a moratorium on the production of fissile material before the conclusion of the FMCT.

On 26 December 1998, Mr Sartaj Aziz, the then Foreign Minister of Pakistan, while explaining Pakistan's official stance on the FMCT to the National Assembly, stated that Pakistan wanted a fissile material treaty which would promote both nuclear non-proliferation and nuclear disarmament, as otherwise the treaty would be discriminatory, and, thus, ineffective. He added that Pakistan's second concern was the unequal stockpiles of fissile material existing at the global, regional, and subregional levels.[37]

Earlier, in October 1998, during the Foreign Secretary level talks, Pakistan proposed a Strategic Restraint Regime to India. It

[34] http://www.forisb.org/nuclear_non_proliferation.html

[35] Resolution 48/75-L was adopted without a vote: see Ambassador Robert T. Grey, Jr., US representative to the Conference on Disarmament, Geneva, 'US Urges Disarmament Conference to Launch Fissile Material Talk', 15 Feb. 2001, http://www.fas.org/nuke/control/fmct/news/treaty-fmct-010215.htm

[36] Ibid.

[37] Afzal Mahmood, 'Pakistan's Stance on FMCT', *Dawn*, 12 Jan. 1999.

encompassed prevention of a nuclear and ballistic missile race, establishment of a risk reduction mechanism, and a proposition that nuclear deterrence should be pursued at the lowest possible level. Unfortunately, India and Pakistan failed in developing convergence on the proposal. Consequently, India rejected it.

On 18 October 2001, Pakistan's Ambassador to the UN at Geneva, Mr Munir Akram, while addressing the UN General Assembly's debate on international peace and security, advocated promotion of nuclear restraint and prevention of the use of nuclear weapons between India and Pakistan. He said that both countries could agree to the following:

1. Formalizing their respective unilateral nuclear test moratoriums, perhaps through a bilateral treaty.
2. Not operationally weaponizing nuclear-capable missile systems.
3. Not operationally deploying nuclear-capable ballistic missiles, and keeping them on de-alert.
4. Formalizing the previous understanding to provide prior and adequate notification of flight tests of missiles.
5. Observing a moratorium on the acquisition, deployment, or development of Anti-Ballistic Missile (ABM) systems.
6. Implementing further confidence building and transparency measures to reduce the risk of the use of nuclear weapons by miscalculation or accident.
7. Open discussions on the nuclear security doctrines of the two countries with a view to forestalling an all-out nuclear arms race.
8. Having an agreement on non-use of force, including the non-use of nuclear weapons.[38]

[38] 'Pakistan Asks UN to Check Indian Designs', *Dawn*, 19 Oct. 2001, http://www.dawn.com/2001/10/19/top3.htm

CHAPTER 3

The Changing Dynamics of the Nuclear Arena

President George W. Bush's strategic framework, the inability of the US to ratify the Comprehensive Test Ban Treaty (CTBT), the new emerging strategic competition between the US and China, the May 1998 nuclear tests by India and Pakistan, the NWS' failure to carry out the obligations of their NPT's Arts. I, IV, and VI, etc., have significantly changed the global non-proliferation and disarmament picture. These developments run counter to widely held beliefs and expectations that the end of the Cold War would make nuclear weapons redundant. Instead, they signal that nuclear weapons could be a growing part of the strategic landscape of the future. They also pose a fundamental problem for the regime based on the NPT. Achieving NPT universality or abolition of nuclear weapons under these circumstances is extremely difficult.

Nuclear status is at the heart of NWS security doctrines, self-awareness, and self-confidence. They have made huge investments of their political credibility, scientific efforts, and financial resources in developing these deadly arsenals. Their military doctrines signify that both tactical and strategic nuclear weapons are important components in their strategies.[1] For example, according to START I counting rules, the US currently deploys approximately 6,000 strategic nuclear warheads on its strategic triad of land-based

[1] Strategic weapons generally consist of more powerful nuclear warheads deployed on long-range delivery systems (missiles, submarines, and bombers) capable of striking the other side's territory. Tactical nuclear weapons, which generally incorporate less powerful nuclear warheads deployed on shorter-range delivery systems, are intended for battlefield use.

missiles, submarines, and bombers. It is estimated that the US deploys over 1,000 tactical nuclear weapons, and more than 5,000 nuclear weapons in reserve stockpiles. The Russian Federation currently deploys an estimated 5,500 strategic nuclear warheads on its strategic triad of land-based missiles, submarines, and bombers. It deploys an estimated 4,000 tactical nuclear weapons, and is believed to stockpile more than 13,000 strategic and tactical nuclear warheads.[2] Nevertheless, on 24 May 2002, the US and Russia signed the Strategic Offensive Reduction Treaty (also known as the 'Moscow Treaty'). This Accord would require the US and Russia to reduce their deployed strategic nuclear arsenals to less than 2,200 warheads each by the end of 2012.[3]

The nuclear disarmament treaties or agreements between the US and the Russian Federation seem practically immaterial because the Bush administration is committed to continue funding research on modifying existing types of nuclear weapons to enable them to destroy deeply buried and hardened targets. It is also seeking a repeal of a ten-year-old prohibition, known as the Spratt-Furse Amendment, against research and development leading to the production of low-yield nuclear weapons.[4] The repeal of the Spratt-Furse Amendment, certainly, strengthens the concept that nuclear weapons do have a battlefield role.

[2] The bilateral arms reductions treaties between the US and the Russian Federation START I and START II did not require the dismantling of warheads removed from operational service, but the treaties did require the destruction of delivery vehicles (missiles, submarines, and bombers) removed from service, significantly reducing the ability of either side to quickly redeploy reserve warheads: 'Arms Control Association Answers Questions About Bush-Putin Arms Talks', *Arms Control Today*, 13 May 2002, http://www.armscontrol.org/aca/summitqamay02.asp

[3] 'Letter of Transmittal and Article-by-Article Analysis of the Treaty on Strategic Offensive Reduction', *Arms Control Today*, July/Aug. 2002, http://www.armscontrol.org/act/2002_07-08/docjul_aug02.asp

[4] Senator Edward Kennedy (D-MA) stated that the 'bunker buster' currently being researched would have a destructive potential ten times that of the blast that destroyed Hiroshima and could 'spew tons of radioactive waste into the atmosphere, with a devastating plume that could poison huge areas in its path': 'Media Advisory: Senators, Scientists Say Congress Should Reject Bush Administration's Proposals for New Nuclear Weapons', *Arms Control Association E-Update*, 1 May 2003.

Nuclear weapons, according to some strategic analysts, are equalizers which guarantee protection to states with limited resources and inferior conventional armaments against invasions and humiliation by a stronger enemy. Since adversarial relations exist alongside violent confrontations, therefore, constructing scenarios in which NWS would give them up in the near future is not a realistic approach. The policies of the de jure NWS (the US, the Russian Federation, the United Kingdom, France, and China), as well as the de facto NWS (India, Pakistan, and Israel), indicate that the true renunciation of nuclear weapons lies beyond any political agenda.

Despite many efforts by the existing nuclear powers, by a variety of agencies of the UN, and by a myriad of treaty organizations, little has been accomplished to dissuade or prevent proliferation. The NWS have not made meaningful progress towards the goal they agreed to in NPT—of sharp reduction in their nuclear arsenals, with the ultimate aim of nuclear disarmament. For instance, in the 2000 NPT Review Conference, the NWS reiterated their unequivocal undertaking to accomplish the total elimination of their nuclear arsenals, leading to nuclear disarmament, to which all state parties are committed under Art. VI of the NPT.[5] However, they did not provide any tangible time frame for the destruction of their respective nuclear arsenals. While the NWS support the objectives of the NPT, in reality they ignore the directives of the treaty.[6] This is because the primary objective of nuclear non-proliferation agreements/treaties is to discourage the proliferation of nuclear weapons to additional states.

Ironically, the representatives of nuclear powers at the international forums condemn nuclear proliferation, and at the same time *defend their own nuclear weapons programmes*. Both the US and the Russian Federation have a doctrine that if their national

[5] The text of the Final Document Issued by the 2000 NPT Review Conference, 20 May 2000, http://www.usinfo.state.gov/topical/pol/arms/stories/finaldoc.htm

[6] Zafar Nawaz Jaspal, 'NPT in 2000: Challenges Ahead', *Strategic Studies*, vol. XX, no. 4, Autumn 2000, pp. 14–19.

interests should so dictate, they would initiate nuclear war. The reliance of these powers on nuclear weapons for the purpose of their national security makes acquisition of nuclear weapons more attractive to other states. Therefore, global regimes that seek to stop the proliferation of nuclear weapons and other Weapons of Mass Destruction (WMD) are under siege. The nuclear tests by India and Pakistan have shown that not all countries share the view that the usefulness of nuclear weapons is declining. Years of relentless effort has not eliminated the clandestine WMD programmes of the most determined proliferators.

It seems that the recent shift in the US' nuclear strategy would negatively influence the nuclear disarmament process. The commitment of President Bush to deploy a missile defence system capable of defending the US and its allies poses a threat to the current strategic nuclear stability, which rests on a hard-won arms control structure, built up over the last 30 years.[7] On 12 July 2001, US National Security Advisor Condoleezza Rice said, 'To be sure, the Cold War arms control regimes we built up for over four decades were useful for their time. Those elements that are worth preserving today, we will keep. And those arms control ideas or treaties that respond to today's reality and build tomorrow's security, we will advance and support.'[8]

President Bush's strategic framework has the potential to open up a Pandora's box of new international security relationships involving defections from existing regimes, the weakening of non-proliferation norms, and the introduction of new offensive and defensive weapons in the arsenals of other states. The anti-missile defence approach and attitude of denial towards nuclear disarmament makes President Bush's declaration about the unilateral

[7] President Bush and his national security team conclude that credible deterrence can no longer be based solely on the prospect of punishment through massive retaliation. Instead, it must be based on a combination of offensive nuclear and non-nuclear defensive capabilities working together to deny potential adversaries the opportunity and benefits from the threat or use of Weapons of Mass Destruction (WMD) against the US.

[8] Text: National Security Advisor Rice at the National Press Club, 12 July 2001, prepared remarks on Europe, Africa, Russia, missile defence, http://usinfo.state.gov

reduction of US nuclear weapons arsenals ineffective.[9] Moreover, it is contrary to the prevailing theory of nuclear deterrence (Mutual Assured Destruction, or MAD), which relied on mutual vulnerability to nuclear attack.

In order to address the anticipated international opposition to the new US Strategic Framework, President Bush and his national security team have continued the balancing act of mixing talk of unilaterally reducing the US nuclear arsenal, and of taking weapons off hair-trigger alert with the pursuit of a missile defence shield. At the same time, nuclear deterrence remains the cornerstone of the US military posture. It preserves the option of first use against an overwhelming conventional attack or against the threat or use of chemical weapons. Moreover, on 13 June 2002, the US' unilateral withdrawal from the ABM Treaty of 1972, and its boycott of the 11–13 November 2001 UN conference to encourage support for the CTBT, undermine the NNPR, within which the individual treaties are interdependent.[10]

The security dilemma, defined as 'the dynamic in which one state's efforts to increase its security are perceived as being achieved at the expense of another state's security, promoting a spiral of competition that usually manifests in [an] arms race that, ultimately, leads to war'.[11] This action-reaction withdrawal cycle could undermine the bilateral nuclear disarmament process between the Russian Federation and the US, as well as jeopardize multilateral NNPR. The weakness of NNPR would adversely affect

[9] On 5 Nov. 2001, the US voted against a Japanese resolution on nuclear disarmament, which it has supported in years past, specifically because the resolution stressed the importance of taking practical steps to implement Art.VI of the NPT, including continuation of the moratorium on nuclear weapon test explosions, etc.: Daryl G. Kimball, 'CTBT Rogue State?', *Arms Control Today*, Dec. 2001.

[10] The nuclear non-proliferation regime is an integrated network of treaties and other standard-setting arrangements which provide a comprehensive framework for the behaviour of states, international organizations, and other actors in the nuclear area: see John Simpson and Darryl Howlett, 'The NPT Renewal Conference : Stumbling Toward 1995', *International Security*, vol. 19, no. 1, Summer 1994, pp. 43–4.

[11] Geoffrey Wiseman, *Concepts of Non-Provocative Defense: Ideas and Practices in International Security*, New York: Palgrave, 2002, p. 3.

horizontal proliferation by making it much easier for threshold states to claim nuclear status. The horizontal as well as vertical proliferation would further increase the problem of safety and security of nuclear arsenals in the international set-up.

The impact of Bush's strategic framework on nuclear weapons proliferation would be different from its impact on ballistic missiles proliferation. The proponents of Ballistic Missile Defence (BMD) one of the opinon that deployment of BMD with a high interception probability may lower states' incentives in possessing or increasing ballistic missiles. In reality, however, it cannot erode the credibility of nuclear deterrence. It would only undermine the credibility of ballistic missiles as effective delivery systems.

States would find delivery means other than ballistic missiles for WMD. Consequently, the search for new strategies would lead to 'Asymmetric Warfare'. Wyn Q. Bowen argued that the approaches to asymmetry include: '... the threat or use of nuclear, biological, and chemical (NBC) weapons; threats or acts of terrorism; the use of propaganda and disinformation; and information attacks against military and civilian computer networks'.[12]

The US BMD plan has raised deep concern in China. Chinese officials and analysts maintain that the US BMD system is primarily intended to counter China's small force of intercontinental ballistic missiles, rather than rogue states.[13] Therefore, deployment of BMD will lessen the effectiveness of China's nuclear deterrence, thus causing China to develop more sophisticated weapons. Modernization and increase of Chinese missiles will prompt India to enhance the size and sophistication of its offensive and defensive ballistic missile capabilities. This will undermine the nuclear deterrence of Pakistan and render it vulnerable

[12] Wyn Q. Bowen, 'The Dimensions of Asymmetric Warfare', in Andrew Dorman, Mike Smith, and Matthew Uttley, eds., *The Changing Face of Military Power: Joint Warfare in an Expeditionary Era*, New York: Palgrave, 2002, pp. 15, 16.

[13] Shannon N. Kile, 'Nuclear Arms Control and Ballistic Missile Defense', *SIPRI Yearbook 2001: Armaments, Disarmament and International Security*, London: Oxford University Press, 2001, p. 442.

to the offensive might of India. This vulnerability will compel Pakistan to enhance the size and sophistication of its nuclear arsenal.

Since the May 1998 nuclear explosions, there has been a renewed chorus of calls from the US, G-8 and other Western states exhorting Pakistan to roll back its nuclear programme and sign the NPT as a non-NWS. On 6 June 1998, the UN Security Council adopted Resolution 1172, which invited Pakistan in conjunction with other states that have not yet done so, to become party to the NPT and CTBT without delay and without conditions.[14]

So long as the global nuclear environment remains similar to what it is now, Pakistan would not move in the opposite direction, viz. denuclearization. It is because of India's traditional stance that the status of nuclear weaponry is a global rather than a regional problem and this in turn determines the direction, level, and patterns of both India's and Pakistan's future nuclear policy. Ashley J. Tellis rightly wrote that as long as Indian decision-makers perceive that the existing nuclear weapons states either will not or cannot move towards significant stockpile reductions that will ultimately lead to nuclear abolition, India will not consider rolling back its own nuclear programme.[15] In such a scenario then, India would not alter its nuclear policy. Similarly, Pakistan too, would not succumb to any pressure for denuclearization as long as India refuses to move in a similar direction first.

The US has been asking India and Pakistan to exercise nuclear restraint. It is likely that Washington will place non-proliferation issues on the back-burner, given its perceptions of India's strategic worth, and Pakistan's need in countering terrorism post-11 September 2001. The US non-proliferation objectives in South Asia will remain secondary to other perceived political, strategic, and commercial goals. Ignoring the pressing need for more

[14] Resolution 1172 (1998), adopted by the Security Council at its 3890th meeting on 6 June 1998, http://www.un.org/Docs/scres/1998/sres1172.htm

[15] Ashley J. Tellis, *India's Emerging Nuclear Posture: Between Recessed Deterrent and Ready Arsenal*, Washington, D.C.: Rand, 2001, p. 21.

effective policy directions and influential strategies to contain South Asian nuclear proliferation, the White House seems bent on repeating earlier mistakes. Perceived US strategic interests have taken precedence over US non-proliferation goals. Consequently, in the post-11 September environment, engagement with the US resulted in the end of nuclear sanctions against India and Pakistan.

CHAPTER 4

Why NRRM and NRR in South Asia?

India and Pakistan have had long standing disputes and conflicts along all their common borders—international, working boundary, and LOC. The nuclear weapons capabilities of both states have further affected the security environment of the region and the possibility of unauthorized use of nuclear weapons, nuclear accidents, etc., has undermined the security of South Asia to a considerable degree. The following are some important issues due to which we need serious discussion for the NRRM and NRR in South Asia.

NUCLEAR WEAPONS: A POLITICIZED ISSUE IN INDIA AND PAKISTAN

Domestic politics have always been an important determinant in Indian and Pakistani nuclear-related decision making.[1] Prime Minister Vajpayee like his predecessor, late Prime Minister Indira Gandhi, manipulated India's nuclear programme for narrow domestic political gains. W.P.S. Sidhu wrote that the May 1974 nuclear test was used to bolster Mrs Indira Gandhi's position by representing it as a major achievement for India, which in turn was identified with the then ruling Congress party.[2] Likewise,

[1] For the detailed causes of South Asian nuclearization, see Zafar Nawaz Jaspal, 'Kashmir: A Nuclear Flash Point', in Azizan, ed., *Nuclear Developments in South Asia and the Future of Global Arams Control*, Wellington: Centre for Strategic Studies, 2001, pp. 12–18.

[2] W.P.S. Sidhu, 'India's Security and Nuclear Risk-Reduction Measures', in Sidhu, Cloughley, Hawes, and Schaffer, *Nuclear Risk-Reduction Measures in South Asia*, Report no. 26, Washington, D.C.: Henry L. Stimson Center, Nov. 1998, p. 8.

Mr Vajpayee used nuclear weapons tests for increasing his own and the BJP's popularity. Praful Bidwai, another Indian analyst, supported this assertion by stating, 'The real impetus for crossing the (nuclear) threshold was domestic, related to the rise of Hindu chauvinist nationalism and the coming to power of the right wing of the BJP-led government in 1998.'[3]

In Pakistan, the popular consensus is that nuclear weapons capability provides credible security against India. In sofar as nuclear weapons, they feel, establish strategic equilibrium between India and Pakistan. Consequently, any increase in military might reduces the risk of aggression and attack. For this reason any change in nuclear policy is totally unacceptable to the Pakistani people and even a slight change would lead to a political backlash for the ruling elite. Every government in Pakistan is conscious of this and therefore very careful in its nuclear-related decision making.

The jingoistic feelings of the masses in India and Pakistan, the non-existence of formal nuclear arms control and disarmament agreements between them, and above all the political use of the nuclear factor in both states endangers the security of South Asia. Thus, any serious move regarding nuclear risk reduction in the region is viewed in both states as a threat to their security.

CENTRALITY OF NUCLEAR WEAPONS IN THE SECURITY DEBATE

Since the overt nuclearization of India and Pakistan, nuclear weapons have occupied centre stage in the India-Pakistan defence and security debates. The centrality of nuclear weapons in strategic discourse has changed strategic thinking entirely in the region and led many observers to believe that the India-Pakistan dispute over Kashmir would perforce get frozen, as neither country would risk a confrontation that could escalate to the nuclear level. How wrong this assumption turned out to be is apparent in the Kargil conflict in 1999 and again the ten-month eyeball-to-eyeball confrontation of 2002 at the India-Pakistan border.

Both countries have commissioned their short and medium-

[3] Praful Bidwai, *Dawn*, 13 May 1999.

range nuclear-capable ballistic missiles with their armies and the deployment of these certainly, poses severe consequential security risks given the relatively short distances between major population centres in India and Pakistan, and the brief time required for missiles to travel such distances. This factor will compress decision-making cycles for national leaders and battlefield commanders, reducing stability during times of crisis.

Although, it is too early to come to a definitive judgement as to whether and how the nuclear factor has shaped the relationship of the two countries, tentative assessments can nevertheless be made. For instance, the nuclear factor appears to have worked both ways in encouraging crisis (limited border wars), and also helping to curb it (by countering developments that could cause escalation to an all-out conventional war, ending up with a nuclear exchange). The so-called nuclear balance of terror—constantly threatening peace in the region—does not deter low-intensity conflicts and limited border wars between India and Pakistan. In other words, any factor that increases the chances of nuclear weapons being used can be considered to be destabilizing.

KASHMIR: A NUCLEAR FLASHPOINT

The absence of an effective conflict resolution mechanism and dispute over the Kashmir region between India and Pakistan has sparked two wars in the past.[4] The nuclear weapon capabilities, the intensity of violence in Indian-held Kashmir, and reinforcing hard-line positions in New Delhi and Islamabad strengthen the argument that the chronic Kashmir conflict could trigger a nuclear war in the subcontinent. Richard Nixon wrote: 'Nuclear powers have never fought each other, but the clash between Muslim Pakistan and Hindu India over the disputed Kashmir territory could erupt into the world's first war between nuclear powers.'[5]

There is a general assumption among strategic thinkers that faced with invasion and military humiliation by India in a fourth

[4] Some analysts refer to the 1999 Kargil conflict as a fourth war between India and Pakistan. Strictly speaking, it wasn't a total war.

[5] Richard Nixon, *Seize the Moment: America's Challenge in a One-Superpower World*, New York: Simon & Schuster, 1992, pp. 21, 22.

war, Islamabad might well resort to nuclear weapons. In an article 'On the Nuclear Edge' (1993), Seymour M. Hersh quotes Richard J. Kerr, Deputy Director of the Central Intelligence Agency in 1990, as saying: 'It was the most dangerous nuclear situation we have ever faced since I've been in the US government. It may be as close as we've come to a nuclear exchange. It was far more frightening than the Cuban missile crisis.' Robert M. Gates, President Bush's deputy national security adviser in 1990, reportedly told Hersh that 'Pakistan and India seemed to be caught in a cycle that they couldn't break out of. I was convinced that if a war started, it would be nuclear.'[6] Bruce Riedel, who was senior adviser to Bill Clinton on India and Pakistan, wrote that the Pakistan Army mobilized its nuclear arsenals against India in July 1999.[7] To the contrary, a number of senior Pakistan Army officials have categorically denied Riedel's assertion.[8]

However, the restraint and maturity shown by India and Pakistan in the 1999 Kargil crisis, and again in the prolonged engagement in 2002 signifies that both states are responsible nuclear states. Simultaneously, every border skirmish between them now carries the potential—however remote—of catastrophic escalation and at the LOC such skirmishes are a daily fact of life.[9] It is possible that Kargil will not be the last crisis between India and Pakistan. Lt. Gen. Kamal Matinuddin (retd) pointed out that 'nuclear deterrence by itself does not ensure peace between

[6] Seymour M. Hersh, 'On the Nuclear Edge', *New Yorker*, 29 Mar. 1993, pp. 56–73. The quotations are on pp. 56–57. This reference was taken from the endnotes of Devin T. Hagerty, 'Nuclear Deterrence in South Asia: The 1990 Indo-Pakistani Crisis', *International Security*, vol. 20, no. 3, Winter 1995, http://www.mtholyoke.edu/acad/intrel/sasianuk.htm

[7] Masood Haider, 'Army Kept PM in Dark', *Dawn*, 14 May 2002; see also Chidanand Rajghatta, 'Musharraf Brought Region to Brink of Nuclear War', *Times of India*, 16 May 2002.

[8] The author interviewed a few Army officers who were engaged in the Kargil conflict. The consensus was that 'there was no such situation when the Indian Army crossed the line of control during the Kargil crisis'. In other words, no grave situation was aroused when nuclear weapons usage became inevitable.

[9] Jonah Blank, 'Kashmir: Fundamentalism Takes Root', *Foreign Affairs*, vol. 78, no. 6, Nov./Dec. 1999, pp. 36–53.

hostile neighbors unless the root cause of possible conflicts is removed'.[10] The dispute over Kashmir could be a tinderbox and a flashpoint for a nuclear conflagration.

LIMITED BORDER WAR: CHALLENGE TO NUCLEAR STABILITY

The continued emphasis on planning for a conventional war is an indication that military planners on both sides have little confidence in nuclear stability. There has been a general consensus among many Indian and Pakistani defence analysts that limited war remains a distinctly possible scenario, and the country that is able to manage the dynamics of a limited war would have a definite advantage. According to former Indian Army Chief Gen. V.P. Malik: '. . . having crossed the nuclear threshold does not mean that a conventional war is out. Nuclear deterrence only restricts an all-out war employing weapons of mass destruction. As a military strategist, I will say that if [the] military grows too big, the initiator, i.e. Pakistan and the affected nation, i.e. India, are tempted to use conventional weapons.'[11]

The ability to fight and win a limited war where nuclear weapons are not allowed to enter the equation is likely to be the hallmark of successful national strategy in future, feels Jasjit Singh.[12] Since the end of the Kargil conflict, Indian strategic pundits have been debating the practicability of limited border war strategy. The Indian military exercise Poorna Vijay (Complete Victory) of summer 1998 was a continuation of this strategic mindset. The officially stated purpose of the exercise was to evaluate concepts and practice battle procedures during offensive and defensive operations on future battlefields, with a nuclear backdrop. Therefore, the exercise was an attempt by India to legitimize conventional war waged under a nuclear umbrella.

This limited border war strategy is equally attractive to some

[10] Lt. Gen. Kamal Matinuddin (retd), *Nuclear Pakistan—Impact on Geopolitical and Regional Environment*, Margalla Papers, no. 2, Dec. 1998, pp. 1–8.

[11] *News*, 11 Feb. 1999.

[12] Jasjit Singh, 'Pakistan's Future War', *Strategic Analysis*, Aug. 1999, pp. 685–702.

Pakistani security analysts. In a limited war confined to one theatre of war, Pakistan's inferiority in conventional weapons and manpower has never been much of a disadvantage. For instance, Pakistan did well against India when the two clashed in the Rann of Kutch in 1965, and in Kashmir in the prelude to the 1965 war, as well as during the 1948 war. Pakistan's smaller size becomes a disadvantage only in the event of an all-out conventional war with India as in 1965 and in 1971. Dr Shireen M. Mazari argued, 'Such a nuclear deterrence/defence will allow Pakistan the flexibility to engage in limited military encounters with India and compel India to keep such engagement limited.'[13]

It seems that both the Indian and Pakistani strategists who are in favour of a limited (local) border war underestimate the likelihood of a surprise strike or escalation of a limited war under a nuclear overhang. Such policies and exercises have a serious military intent and message. The lethal cross-border artillery duels, rising casualties, sharpened tempers, and deepening antagonism may collectively escalate a limited border war to an all-out conventional war, and then possibly to a nuclear confrontation. While commenting on nuclear deterrence in South Asia, Strobe Talbot stated: 'We hope they will look at the record again, not from the vantage point of having seen the Cold War end peacefully, but rather from the hard-headed perspective of what it took to manage the rivalry. The US and the Soviet Union had more than one narrow escape. India and Pakistan have even fewer margins for error than the US and the USSR over Cuba and Berlin, if only for geographical reasons, since no ocean separates them.'[14]

Seeking a war in the belief that use of nuclear weapons can be isolated from it shows a lack of understanding of the escalatory dynamic built into military campaigns. That Pakistan's leadership could think of Kargil as a feasible military option without a nuclear risk demonstrated a dangerous propensity to risk-taking. The

[13] Shireen M. Mazari, *Nuclearization of South Asia: The Geopolitical Dimension*, Margalla Papers, no. 2, Dec. 1998, pp. 9–26.

[14] Strobe Talbot, 'US Looks to India's Emergence as a Global Power', *Times of India*, 13 Nov. 1998.

Indian leadership's belief in war being an option and its discounting of the nuclear dangers is equally risk-prone.[15]

UNENDING SIACHEN GLACIER CONFLICT

India and Pakistan have been interlocked in a costly struggle in Kashmir's Siachen Glacier area. Since the winter of 1983–4, the two nations have battled over a 2,500-sq. km. triangle of contested territory. This is claimed to be the world's highest battleground (16,000–20,000 ft. above sea level). The dispute arose over different interpretations of provisions of the 1949 ceasefire, as well as the subsequent 1972 Simla Agreement, which left a portion of the ceasefire line (CFL) undefined.

The line of actual control drawn up under the Simla Agreement (1972) left out the glacier region because delineation was considered impracticable. The boundary was delineated only up to map coordinate NJ9842 and vaguely referenced the direction from there as 'thence north to the glaciers', leaving a distance of about 65 km. undemarcated and disputed, but untouched.[16]

Since 1947, Pakistan had administered the area and authorized international mountaineering expeditions into the glacier region from 1957 to 1983. After a series of secret military expeditions, India moved in its forces in 1983–4 winter, occupying the Sia La, Belafond La, and Gyongla passes of the Saltoro range lying west and adjacent to the Siachen Glacier.[17] Since April 1984, the Pakistani forces halted Indian advances and have been fighting to recapture the occupied zone. Several rounds of talks to disengage the forces over the glacier have not produced any results, till the time of writing this. Fortunately, both sides have refrained from expanding this theatre of limited war into all-out war. For sustaining this war, both neighbours have been paying a heavy cost

[15] V. R. Raghavan, 'India's Nuclear Balance Sheet', *Hindu*, 7 May 2002.

[16] Shirin Tahir Kheli and Kent L. Biringer, *Reducing Risk in South Asia: Managing India-Pakistan Tensions*, CMC Occasional Papers, US: Sandia National Laboratories, Mar. 2001, p. 10.

[17] Rasul B. Rais, 'Pakistan in the Regional and Global Power Structure', *Asian Survey*, vol. XXXI, no. 4, Apr. 1991, pp. 378–92.

in terms of casualties of troops and economics. For example, the cost of fighting is conservatively estimated at $200 million annually for India, and at least half that amount for Pakistan, with its easier lines of communication and access.[18]

The ongoing Siachen Glacier conflict, nevertheless, needs serious all out effort if it is to be resolved since it is a source of constant tension in the region.

DIVERGENT VIEWS ON NO-FIRST-USE OF NUCLEAR WEAPONS PROPOSAL

Pakistan feels thaeatened by an adversary and a neigbour which is several times larger. The situation is somewhat identical to the European theatre vis-à-vis the former Soviet Union during the Cold War. Pakistan, therefore feels the need for a defensive fence against India in order to preserve its territorial integrity and independence. Pakistan's geographical narrowness or lack of strategic depth and India's commitment to introducing more sophisticated nuclear-capable delivery systems, like cruise missile and ballistic missile defence systems are perceived as serious threats.

Pakistan's nuclear weapons are for deterring conventional as well as nuclear aggression against it. It announced that its nuclear weapons would be the instruments of last resort against any future Indian military adventure and abandoned the No-First-Use (NFU) policy in its nuclear strategy. In simple words, it means that Pakistan has a first-use policy on nuclear weapons: that is, Pakistan will not hesitate to use nuclear weapons if faced with a sufficiently threatening conventional defeat of its armed forces.[19]

Adopting an NFU policy by Pakistan would mean that con-

[18] Ibid.

[19] This is similar to the American policy of 'Flexible Response' enunciated by US Secretary of Defense Robert McNamara in 1962 that 'the US is also prepared to counter with nuclear weapons any Soviet conventional attack so strong that it cannot be dealt with conventional means': Gaurav Rajen, 'Tactical Nuclear Weapons in South Asia: The Need to Disavow Development and Deployment', *Disarmament Forum*, United Nations: UNIDR, Four, 2002, p. 59.

ventional war could be fought between India and Pakistan that would probably not involve nuclear weapons. It would not only encourage, but also strengthen the argument of the Indian strategic pundits, who believe in achieving certain objectives by limited conventional war. However, official discussions in Pakistan indicate that Pakistani policy makers lack belief in India's NFU undertaking in its nuclear doctrine draft. According to Sir Michael Quinlan:

> NFU promises can bé no more than peacetime political theatre. They cannot change the reality of what would be fearfully difficult and stressful situations, if they have any security effect at all. Meanwhile, it can only be in the direction of marginally diluting the war-prevention effect of nuclear weapons in deterrence, and in ultimate security matters, I do not believe in political theatre.[20]

Therefore, Islamabad has made it clear on several occasions that it would cross the nuclear threshold in a war against India to prevent India's numerically superior army from invading.

DIVERGENT VIEWS ON NO-WAR PACT BETWEEN INDIA AND PAKISTAN

Pakistan had proposed a No-War Pact and an agreement on mutual and balanced reduction of forces and armaments. India rejected this submission. Analysts of a No-War Pact exacerbated the potential for unwanted use of nuclear weapons and the decapitation threats of nuclear weapons. Therefore, it seems that Pakistan would develop a strong incentive to posture its nuclear forces for early use in a crisis, before its nuclear option was curtailed or eliminated by enemy attack.

India would have a similar incentive to strike first, to maximize its chances for destroying the target arsenal before it could be

[20] Michael Quinlan, 'The Development of NATO Nuclear Doctrine', *Journal of the United Service Institution of India*, vol. CXXX, no. 540, Apr.–June 2000, pp. 285–6.

used. Thus, the decapitation problem provides strong incentives to adopt launch-on-warning postures.[21] Launch-on-warning postures are very prone to accidental and unauthorized use.

VULNERABILITY OF NUCLEAR FACILITIES

Nuclear accidents or illicit trafficking of fissile material in India or the Russian Federation[22] is enough to highlight that the safety and security of nuclear facilities and arsenals has become an important global problem. According to the *Washington Post*, after an October 2002 briefing on Al Qaeda's nuclear ambitions by CIA Director George Tenet, President Bush '. . . ordered his national security team to give nuclear terrorism priority over every other threat to the United States'.[23]

Praful Bidwai claimed: 'Both Pakistan and India have a poor culture of safety and high rates of mishaps in their Armed Forces establishment. Their nuclear programmes have an embarrassingly bad safety record.'[24] His apprehension seems accurate to some extent. For instance, on 27 August 2001, the Indian police in West Bengal arrested two men with more than 200 gm. of semi-processed Uranium.[25] On 23 July 1998, India's Central Bureau of Intelligence seized 6 kg. of Uranium from G.R. Arun, a city engineer, and S. Murthy, his associate, in Tamil Nadu. Scientists at the Indira Gandhi Centre for Atomic Research (IGCAR) at Kalpakkam stated that the seized Uranium was capable of radia-

[21] Tariq Rauf, 'Nuclear and Missile CBMs in South Asia', in Dipankar Banerjee, ed., *Confidence Building Measures in South Asia*, Colombo: Regional Centre for Strategic Studies, p. 136.

[22] Jessica Stern, *The Ultimate Terrorists*, London: Harvard University Press, 2000, p. 97; also see 'Uranium Racket Unearthed', Press Trust of India, 24 July 1998, http://www.indian-express.com/ie/daily/19980724/20550804.html

[23] Tom Z. Collina and Jon B. Wolfsthal, 'Nuclear Terrorism and Warhead Control in Russia', *Arms Control Today*, Apr. 2002, http://www.armscontrol.org/act/2002_04/colwolfapril02.asp

[24] Praful Bidwai, 'Nuclear Chickens Come Home', *Frontline*, vol. 18, issue 23, 10–23 Nov. 2001, http://www.flonnet.com/fl1823/18230180.htm

[25] Shireen M. Mazari and Maria Sultan, *Nuclear Safety and Terrorism: A Case Study of India*, Islamabad Papers, no. 19, 2001, p. 6.

tion emission, having energy corresponding to natural U-238 and U-235.[26] It seems that a nuclear mafia is operating in India.

Two Pakistani nuclear scientists, Sultan Bashir-ud-Din Mehmood and Abdul Majid, were detained on suspicion of sharing technical information with Osama bin Laden. After investigation, they were subsequently released. No illicit traffic of Pakistan's nuclear material and nuclear accident had occurred or reported till the writing of these lines. On 19 October 2002, the then Information Minister of Pakistan, Mr Nisar Memon, said, 'Pakistan's strategic assets have been secure since the nuclear programme started and, thank God, there has been no leakage of any kind.' He added, 'Nobody will ever be able either to attack or take them away.'[27] This is an indication that the Government of Pakistan is conscious of the safety and security of its nuclear weapons and fissile materials.

However, in India, there have been many cases of theft of medical isotopes and other sources of radiation. These incidents are often overlooked because radioisotopes cannot be used to make detonable devices. But one cannot rule out the use of these isotopes in Radiological Dispersal Devices (RDDs). Terrorists could use them as 'weapons of mass disruption' to draw attention to their cause, to wreak havoc, and to terrorize civilians.

There are a number of nuclear medical and agriculture research centres in both countries and often these are located inside or near urban centres. Despite the Indian and Pakistani governments' assurances and claims that they are aware of the importance of mantaining security of their nuclear infrastructure, it is apparant that these civilian nuclear facilities often have little security, even if they are dealing with hundreds of kilograms of radioactive material. The proximity of civilian nuclear facilities to population centres and their simple and fragile security arrangements might encourage terrorists to use them for their nefarious designs.

[26] 'Uranium Racket Unearthed', Press Trust of India, 24 July 1998, http://www.indian.express.com/ie/daily/19980724/20550804.html

[27] 'Pakistan will Keep Nukes out of Extremists' Hands: Nisar', *Dawn*, 20 Oct. 2002.

NUCLEAR ACCIDENTS

Another frightening possibility that could easily translate into reality is the risk of a nuclear accident caused by human, mechanical or electronic error. Both India and Pakistan lack the experience and sophisticated security systems necessary to guard against human miscalculation and mechanical error.

The Indian nuclear facilities are vulnerable to a high probability of accidents. According to an Indian parliamentary report, 147 mishaps or unusual safety-related occurrences were reported between 1995 and 1998 in Indian atomic energy plants.[28] On 4 January 2001, a Milan missile (an anti-tank weapon, capable of carrying a nuclear warhead) fired accidentally in the presence of the then Defence Secretary, Mr Yogendra Narain, at the Bharat Dynamics Limited. It left one quality control officer for the Milan missile programme dead and injured five others at the unit. This unit is located in a thickly populated part of Hyderabad city. T. Lalith Singh commented, 'Even as the accidental missile firing at the Bharat Dynamics Limited here continues to be shrouded in mystery, several questions are raised over the safety procedures adopted at the country's premier missile production unit.'[29]

Western analysts view Pakistan's nuclear facilities as accident-prone too, but it has so far successfully prevented nuclear accidents in its facilities. To improve its safety and security mechanisms, Pakistan joined certain nuclear-related treaties and several other proposals made over the years. On 4 September 2000, Pakistan ratified the Convention on the Physical Protection of Nuclear Material (1979). Pakistan is also party to the Convention on Early Notification of a Nuclear Accident and Nuclear Safety Convention. The international Convention on Nuclear Safety envisages complete separation between the regulatory and promotional aspects of nuclear energy. Accordingly, in January 2001, the Government of Pakistan promulgated the PNRA Ordinance, establishing a completely independent regulatory authority called the Pakistan Nuclear Regulatory Authority (PNRA). This

[28] Mazari and Sultan, op. cit., n. 25 above, p. 9.

[29] T. Lalith Singh, 'Doubts over BDL Safety Norms', *Hindu*, 9 Jan. 2001.

authority has been entrusted with the control, regulation and supervision of all matters related to nuclear safety and radiation protection measures in Pakistan. Despite these arrangements, the international community has doubts about the safety and security of Pakistan's nuclear infrastructure.

COMMAND, CONTROL, COMMUNICATION AND INTELLIGENCE STRUCTURE: CHALLENGES

Of all the factors shaping India-Pakistan strategic relations in the present environment, none is potentially more important than Command, Control, Communication and Intelligence (C3I). The sensors, communications systems, operational procedures, and command organizations that comprise, in effect, the central nervous systems of the Indian and Pakistani defence establishments play a critical role in security. They determine the responsiveness of nuclear forces to each other—and to their respective national authorities—in peacetime, in crisis, and in conflict. Despite the importance of C3I, however, neither India nor Pakistan is likely to have access to sophisticated C3I components in the foreseeable future.

Even if they would be available to them, it would not make much difference, since the flight time of missiles between India and Pakistan ranges from between 3 and 11 minutes. Therefore, in spite of having advanced C3I capabilities, neither would discover it had been nuked until after the fact. Moreover, the command centres of both states are dangerously vulnerable to attack. This vulnerability might tempt a pre-emptive strike in a crisis. Thus, an all-out nuclear exchange could be sparked by a misinterpretation of intentions, or by the accidental use of nuclear weapon between India and Pakistan.

UNAUTHORIZED USE

Unauthorized use can take place if those who are tasked with using the weapons under authorized conditions have the ability to use them regardless of whether they are given an authoritative order. The possibility of unauthorized use becomes more acute when a state delegates control of its nuclear weapons to the local commanders and disperses them in order to increase the survivability of its strategic assets. There is a possibility that India and Pakistan in all likelihood move towards delegated control and dispersal to increase the survivability of their nuclear assets—India vis-à-vis China, and Pakistan vis-à-vis India. By this strategy, both India and Pakistan would offset conventional asymmetries and respectively compensate for their lack of strategic depths.

The first line of defence against unauthorized activation is a lock on the weapon. The earliest locks were mechanical combination locks. Two different codes are inserted, simultaneously or almost simultaneously. This is the 'two-man rule', which means that it becomes impossible to arm any nuclear weapon through the actions of a single individual. The codes are usually changed on a regular schedule.[30] Since the early 1960s, the US especially has increasingly employed a more sophisticated system called a Permissive Action Link (PAL). A PAL is an electronic (originally electro-mechanical) device that prevents arming the weapon unless the correct codes are inserted into it.[31] India and Pakistan do not possess PAL technology.

This problem would assume alarming proportions when India and Pakistan maintain their nuclear weapons on a hair trigger alert or launch on warning operational stage. Currently, India and Pakistan are observing a policy of nuclear restraint. Their official stance is that the nuclear warheads have been kept as separate components, not as assembled warheads. The fact that they are kept unassembled at different locations, makes scientific

[30] 'Principles of Nuclear Weapons Security and Safety', http://www.fas.org/nuke/hew/Usa/Weapons/Pal.html

[31] The traditional nuclear powers have developed highly sophisticated technologies to eliminate accidental or unauthorized use of nuclear weapons. The US was probably the leader with Permissive Action Links (PALs), the electronic locks that went through four stages of upgradation and improvement of dependability features. France and Russia had versions of their own. The British had the technology but relied more on human arrangements that made final decisions dependent on cooperative action by many highly competent individuals: Tanvir Ahmad Khan, 'A Command and Control System', *Dawn*, 15 Feb. 2000.

expertise essential for assembly.[32] India's draft nuclear doctrine reveals that it would operationalize its nuclear potential. Islamabad will also follows in case that happens. If these warheads are indeed deployed, both India and Pakistan require expertise about the dual code or key systems and PAL, which are essential for protection against unauthorized use.

India and Pakistan have no access to PAL technology, and also lack other related expertise. These drawbacks increase the risk of unstable civilian or military officers getting control of a nuclear weapon and using it. This is a possibility that cannot be ignored. It is imperative, therefore that the Indian and Pakistani Command and Control Systems controlling dispersed, concealed, and mobile launchers devise reliable mechanisms to eliminate unauthorized use in a crisis situation.

IRRATIONAL LEADER AND COMMAND AND CONTROL ARRANGEMENTS

The possibility also exists that the person exercising the highest political authority might himself/herself behave irrationally.[33] Human error, egotism, mechanical breakdowns, and factional struggles can derail methodical decision-making. To counter this kind of situation, an infalliable strategy is required in the form of a command and control institution. Institutionalization of command and control in both India and Pakistan is in a preliminary stage at present.

[32] President Pervez Musharraf stated, 'Pakistan's nuclear weapons are not ready to be fired, they are not mated, they are geographically apart and they are not in a condition in which a button has to be pressed to fire them'. See 'Pak Nukes Not Ready to be Fired: President', *News*, 11 Nov. 2001.

[33] Many famous leaders throughout history were psychotic or experienced psychotic episodes: Caligula, Nero, Ludwig of Bavaria, and probably Adolf Hitler and Joseph Stalin as well. Woodrow Wilson and Dwight Eisenhower suffered serious strokes while in office, which compromised their ability to perform their duties and think clearly. During his final days before resigning the presidency in 1974, Richard Nixon is said to have acted irrationally under the stress of the Watergate scandal. See David P. Barash, *Introduction to Peace Studies*, California: Wadsworth, 1991, p. 125.

On 2 February 2000, Pakistan announced the formation of its National Command Authority (NCA). The NCA comprises an Employment Control Committee, a Development Control Committee, and a Strategic Plans Division, which will act as the secretariat. The apex Employment Control Committee would be chaired by the head of government and include the Minister of Foreign Affairs (as Deputy Chairman), Minister of Defence, Minister of Interior, the Chairman of the Joint Chiefs of Staff Committee, the Services Chiefs, the Director General of the Strategic Plans Division, and technical advisers and others, as required by the Chairman.[34] The officials in Pakistan have claimed that the NCA arrangement thwarts the possibility of any irrational decision by individual(s). Notably, in the beginning of 2003, the NCA was chaired by the head of the state, President Pervez Musharraf, instead of the head of government, Prime Minister Mir Zafurullah Jamali.

On 4 January 2003, India publicly announced a formal nuclear command structure under civilian control.[35] This made public a set of political principles and administrative arrangements to manage its arsenal of atomic weapons. Although the broad outline of India's nuclear doctrine was already known, the nature and chain of its command and control over nuclear weapons had remained unclear. The Indian Cabinet Committee on Security (CCS), however, did not announce everything. Missing from its statement is the actual composition of the NCA at its political and executive levels.

The CCS also mentions that it has 'reviewed and approved the arrangements for alternate chains of command for retaliatory nuclear strikes in all eventualities'. This is a reference to a situation in which the prime minister may be incapacitated during a

[34] 'National Command Authority Formed', *Dawn*, 3 Feb. 2000.

[35] C. Raja Mohan, 'Nuclear Command Authority Comes into Being', *Hindu*, 5 Jan. 2003, http://www.thehindu.com/stories/2003010504810100.htm; Josy Joseph, 'India sets up Strategic Forces Command', rediff.com, 4 Jan. 2003, http://www.rediff.com/news/2003/jan/04nuke1.htm; and see also Kerry Boyd, 'India Establishes Formal Nuclear Command Structure', *Arms Control Today*, Jan./Feb. 2003.

crisis. But the CCS did not reveal how the power to press the nuclear button would move down the political chain in the event of such a contingency. Importantly, the most acute problem (technological backwardness) exists in the process of succession within the command authority. On the other hand, India lacks the ability to install uninterruptible communications channels between different levels of succession.

POSSIBILITY OF NUCLEAR TERRORISM

Nuclear weapons can be used by terrorists to inflict a huge number of casualities in any future activities they decide to embark upon. The chemical nerve agent used in a terrorist attack by the Aum Shinri Kyo cult in Tokyo in 1995 has been widely viewed as the crossing of a threshold. This theory is reinforced by evidence uncovered recently to the effect that non-state actors (subnational groups or terrorists' organizations) are interested in nuclear, chemical and biological (NBC) weaponry.[36] On 30 November 2002, Russian President Vladimir Putin had expressed the fear that Pakistan's WMD could fall into the hands of 'bandits and terrorists'.[37]

Anthrax, a small sample of which can be called the terrorism of substances (biological and chemical), strengthened the fear that NBC would be used in future terrorist acts. The data in recent years is revealing and indicates that the possibility of using biological and chemical weapons is more than that of nuclear weapons, the reason being the technological problems associated with the manufacture of nuclear weapons. The possibility of the use of nuclear weapons in future terrorist acts cannot be ruled out however because of the established fact of state-sponsored

36 Hamid Mir, 'Osama Claims He Has Nukes: If US Uses N-Arms it Will Get Same Response', *Dawn*, 10 Nov. 2001.

37 'Pak Weapons could Fall into Hands of Terrorists: Putin', *Khaleej Times Online*, 1 Dec. 2002, http://www.khaleejtimes.co.ae/subcont.htm#storyb. See Amit Baruah, 'Concerns over Terrorists Acquiring Pak Nuclear Arms Remain: Putin', *Hindu*, 1 Dec. 2002, http://www.hinduonnet.com/stories/2002120104380100.htm; also see 'Russia Concerned at Pakistan's Nukes', *Dawn*, 2 Dec. 2002.

terrorism. Paul Wilkinson argued that 'many terrorist movements are directly encouraged, sponsored and aided by regimes in order to weaken or subvert rival states'.[38] It is not surprising then that pro-terrorist states assist terrorist organizations by providing nuclear radioactive material because of their close connection between them. The US alleged that an 'axis of evil' has been involved in state-sponsored terrorism. President Bush stated that, in cases of countries of concern, 'terror and blackmail are a way of life'. He added that 'they seek' missiles armed with 'weapons of mass destruction to keep the US and other responsible nations from helping allies and friends in strategic parts of the world'.[39]

Many analysts argue that nuclear weapons are extremely difficult to manufacture. Terrorists groups which have no state support cannot develop them. Repudiating the use of nuclear weapons by terrorists groups because of technical difficulty is an erroneous approach. In fact, the difficult part of making a nuclear bomb is producing the separated Plutonium or HEU. Second, a distinction must be drawn between the kind of military weapons which states strive to develop, and the rougher, crude types of devices which terrorists would be satisfied with. Matthew Bunn wrote: 'Even some particularly well-organized terrorists groups could potentially make at least a crude nuclear bomb if they could get enough of the necessary Plutonium and HEU.'[40] What terrorists require are radiological bombs, in which radioactive materials are packed around a conventional bomb and an incendiary material. With this type of weapon, the explosion leads to a fireball, shooting the radioactive material up into the air, which then

[38] Paul Wilkinson, 'Terrorism: International Dimensions', in William Gutteridge, *The New Terrorism*, London: Mansell Publishing, 1986, p. 29.

[39] Ben Sheppard, 'US Missile Defence Plans Consign ABM Treaty to History, but Where do the Allies Go from Here?', *Jane's Information Group*, 3 May 2001.

[40] The amount of material needed for a bomb is small: 4 kg. of Plutonium and about three times that amount of HEU is potentially enough for a nuclear weapon. See Matthew Bunn, 'A Detailed Analysis of the Urgently Needed New Steps to Control Warheads and Fissile Material', in Joseph Cirincione, ed., *Repairing the Regime: Preventing the Spread of Weapons of Mass Destruction*, New York: Routledge, 2000, p. 74.

falls back to earth, scattering over a wide area. The primary purpose of such weapons is to spread radioactive contamination rather than cause casualties through blast effects.[41]

Nuclear weapons' components and know-how are available in the black market. Hundreds of tons of nuclear material, the essential ingredients of nuclear weapons, are stored at vulnerable sites throughout the former Soviet Union, guarded only by underpaid, hungry, and disheartened people. At least eight thefts of materials (weapons-usable) that could be used to make nuclear weapons have been confirmed.[42] Praful Bidwai claimed: 'Both Pakistan and India have a poor culture of safety and high rates of mishaps in their Armed Forces establishment. Their nuclear programmes have an embarrassingly bad safety record.'[43] His apprehensions seem well founded. For instance, on 27 August 2001, the Indian Police in West Bengal arrested two men with more than 200 grams of semi-processed Uranium.[44] In addition, there are many cases of theft of medical isotopes and other sources of radiation. These incidents are often overlooked, because radioisotopes cannot be used to make detonable nuclear bombs. But terrorists could use them to draw attention to their cause, to wreak havoc, and to terrorize civilians. In both states there are a number of nuclear medical and agriculture research centres located inside or near cities which could be used by terrorists. What this means then is that a nuclear-related dialogue between India and Pakistan is essential and impevative even though since the realization of each other's nuclear weapons potential, an all-out war has been avoided. A steady and consistant dialogue would develop greater understanding of each other's concerns. Communications play an important role in CBMs and bona fide transparency in actions

[41] Nadine Gurr and Benjamin Cole, *The New Face of Terrorism: Threats from Weapons of Mass Destruction*, London: I.B.Tauris, 2000, pp. 44, 45.

[42] Russian officials have repeatedly denied that any case of smuggling involved weapon-grade nuclear material, which, according to the strict definition, is Uranium enriched to more than 90 per cent U-235 or Plutonium with less than 7 per cent Pu-240: Stern, op. cit., n. 22 above, p. 97.

[43] Bidwai, op. cit., n. 24 above.

[44] Mazari and Sultan, op. cit., n. 25 above, p. 6.

will allow both parties to get a better insight of (and even a voice in) what each is doing. Sharing information on future actions is essential to build understanding. A chain of goodwill gestures that could lead to negotiating and solving long standing persistent problems. CBMs, do not mean conflict resolution per se, but do indirectly pave the way for the same.[45] Therefore, NCBMs are imperative for South Asian peace and security and are a part of serious regional security debate. The following discussion reveals the reasoning:

[45] Behzad Shahandeh, 'Confidence Building Measures in the Persian Gulf', *Discourse: Iranian Quarterly*, vol. 2, no. 2, Fall 2000, http://www.netiran.com/Htdocs/Clippings/FPolitics/201209XXFP03.html

CHAPTER 5

Nuclear CBMs: Utilitarian Approach

Since the realization of the immense destructive capabilities of nuclear weapons and recognition that in a nuclear war there is no winner, or the MAD concept, nuclear CBMs have received great importance in the security dialogue among NWS. The CBM endeavour, for example, in the East-West setting can be traced back to the Cuban Missile crisis of 1962. The crisis was a turning point in the East-West relationship in the sense that it was a bolt from the blue for the US and the Western alliance, and its dangers and uncertainties were widely felt by the Soviet leadership as well. The stand-off intensified interest in measures that would bring about greater communication, transparency, predictability, and stability in the strategic and military relationship between the two blocs.[1] Did they, in fact, achieve anything at all? There is a consensus amongst security analysts that CBMs strengthened stability and enhanced international security by institutionalizing channels of communication between adversaries. Significantly, CBMs entered the diplomatic language following the negotiation of some modest measures during the 1975 CSCE Helsinki Conference. The Helsinki Final Act ascribed three basic objectives to CBMs

1. To eliminate the causes of tensions.
2. To promote confidence and contribute to stability and security.
3. To reduce the danger of armed conflict arising from misunderstanding or miscalculation.[2]

[1] Kanti Bajpai, 'CBMs: Contexts, Achievements, Functions', in Dipankar Banerjee, ed., *Confidence Building Measures in South Asia*, Colombo: Regional Centre for Strategic Studies, pp. 9–10.

[2] Moonis Ahmar, 'Rationalizing the Concept of Confidence-Building Measures',

CBMs, by definition, are supposed to be modest steps required in facilitating and ushering in the right environment to avoid new explosions and reduce tensions and also allow the political and military leadership on rival sides to communicate with each other. 'Precisely, CBMs aim to create a situation in which the warring parties agree to take mutual steps for building trust and starting talks for the diffusion of crisis or the resolution of conflict', stated Dr Moonis Ahmar.[3]

Dr Pervaiz Iqbal Cheema, while examining the utility of the CBM process, argued that 'CBMs can take the form of a general understanding between nations and may emerge in the form of a formal agreement.'[4] Thus, CBMs are said to be useful instruments for preventing wars, bringing about arms control and disarmament agreements, and facilitating conflict resolution. It is also suggested that they are applicable to all states, are easily negotiable, and bring only benefits, because they are supposed to improve trust between rival states or potential adversaries, and clear the path to better political and military relations.[5]

Nuclear CBMs laid the foundation of the international NNPR,[6] and reduced the danger of nuclear-armed conflict arising from misunderstanding or miscalculation. Though NNPR has not been successful in completely controlling or eliminating nuclear weapons, yet, it has demonstrated its effectiveness. At the heart of the confidence building-endeavour was the idea of preventing inadvertent or accidental war, limiting wartime escalation should hostilities actually occur, and terminating hostilities short of total war. Through mutual understanding, the five NWS suc-

---

in Moonis Ahmar, ed., *The Challenge of Confidence-Building in South Asia*, New Delhi: Har-Anand Publications, 2001, pp. 39–40.

[3] Ibid.

[4] Pervaiz Iqbal Cheema, 'CBMs and South Asia', in Banerjee, ed., op. cit., n. 1 above, p. 31.

[5] Marie-France Desjardins, *Rethinking Confidence-Building Measures*, Adelphi Paper 307, London: Oxford University Press, Dec. 1996, p. 4.

[6] The international nuclear arms control and disarmament treaties and agreements constitute the nuclear non-proliferation regime.

cessfully managed to avoid nuclear war during the peak of the Cold War and protected their nuclear weapons programmes. Moreover, the NWS maintain their monopoly in the field of nuclear weapons by negotiating and promulgating discriminatory international treaties. In the 1960s, for example, the US, the former USSR, and the UK negotiated the nuclear NPT, which was promulgated in 1970. By virtue of the NPT, the NWS secure their legitimate right to maintain their nuclear weapons arsenals and prohibit the horizontal proliferation of these weapons.

The tangible outcomes of the nuclear CBMs between the Americans and the Russians are impressive. These CBMs have led to the constitution of the 1972 ABM Treaty, followed by the Treaty on the Elimination of Intermediate-Range and Shorter Range Missiles (ground-launched missiles with a range of 500 to 5,500 km). The Strategic Arms Reduction Treaty (START) I and START II Treaties provided significant missile and warhead reductions. Moreover, launch transparency measures were dealt with in, among other things, the Agreement on Measures to Reduce the Risk of Outbreak of Nuclear War (1971), the Agreement on the Prevention of Incidents On and Over the High Seas (1972), Agreement on Notifications of Launches of Intercontinental Ballistic Missiles and Submarine-Launched Ballistic Missiles (1988), Agreement on the Establishment of Nuclear Risk Reduction Centres (1987), and the Memorandum of Understanding regarding the establishment in Moscow of a joint centre for exchange of data from early warning systems and notifications of missile launches.

CHAPTER 6

Debate on Nuclear CBMs in the South Asian Context

As mentioned earlier, the concept of nuclear CBMs was born in the East-West context, with particular emphasis on Europe. During the 1970s and the 1980s, they applied nuclear CBMs to avoid outcomes that would be unfavourable to them, even when they were in a conflictual relationship. Significantly, CBMs do not entail conflict resolution or the orientation of a peace process. CBMs assume that even in heated conflicts, there are many situations that parties in competition (or even deep hostility) would want to avoid. The measures could be preventive or CBMs, and sometimes, a combination of the two. Theoretically, preventive measures could be divorced from CBMs, but in actual fact it is very difficult, since they complement each other.[1]

On 18 May 1974, India conducted its first nuclear test. Since then, unilateral nuclear disarmament or capping of the nuclear weapons programme by either side (India and Pakistan) has not figured as important in the NCBM debate in South Asia. This sort of initiative can be seen as not being genuine, and actually raises doubts about a conspiracy. Furthermore, the nuclear tests in May 1998 make it abundantly clear that India and Pakistan are unlikely to roll back or eliminate their nuclear capabilities. The pro-nuclear lobby in both states criticized the US-led international propaganda against their nuclear weapons capabilities.

While commenting on Western anxiety on South Asian nuclearization, Kapil Kak stated, 'Western fears on the subcontinent being a geo-political flashpoint, articulated with regular frequency, would appear to be part of the spin on their non-

[1] Behzad Shahandeh, 'Confidence Building Measures in the Persian Gulf', *Discourse: Iranian Quarterly*, vol. 2, no. 2, Fall 2000, http://www.netiran.com/Htdocs/Clippings/FPolitics/201209XXFP03.html

proliferation agenda.'[2] In response to some Western scholars' apprehensions, Jasjit Singh asserted that: Western experts and literature have been painting doomsday scenarios of a nuclear war in the subcontinent on the assumptions that both states are less responsible than the developed states who used nuclear weapons and built up arsenals of tens of thousands of nuclear weapons which they are finding so difficult to even reduce.[3]

The NCBMs that do not disturb the nuclear deterrence of either party can be acceptable in the hostile India-Pakistan environment. In fact, CBMs as confidence building steps are intrinsically harmless. They cannot injure the interests of any nation, nor can they be an impediment in the path of national objectives and strategies. To be precise, CBMs are measures to primarily boost mutual confidence. Significantly, the failure of the UN to resolve the Kashmir issue, the prevalent South Asian security environment, and the strategic nuclear equilibrium between India and Pakistan make NCBMs between them imperative for their national interests. The national interests of both neighbours make it obligatory that they seriously develop understanding intended for avoiding a situation detrimental to their bilateral relations. Brahma Chellaney believes that, The bilateral approach remains the best for tackling bilateral differences and problems, even as embryonic efforts to evolve a regional framework for security issues.... The bilateral approach provides the most direct method to articulate national interests, resolve disputes peacefully, and deter potential aggression....[4]

In retrospect, there is a long list of nuclear-related initiatives on CBMs in South Asia. Pakistan proposed most of them. In fact, Pakistan supports all equitable and multilateral measures to control the spread of nuclear weapons. Nevertheless, Pakistan has ruled out any unilateral decision regarding the fate of a country's

[2] Kapil Kak, 'India's Conventional Defence Problems and Prospects', *Strategic Analysis*, vol. XXII, no. 11, Feb. 1999, pp. 1639–65.

[3] Jasjit Singh, 'Arms Race in the Region: Myths and Reality', *Strategic Analysis*, vol. XVIII, no. 5, Aug. 1995, pp. 595–609.

[4] Brahma Chellaney, 'CBMs: A Critical Appraisal', in Dipankar Banerjee, ed., *Confidence Building Measures in South Asia*, Colombo: Regional Centre for Strategic Studies, p. 24.

nuclear programme. It is believed that the regional approach to non-proliferation and disarmament is complementary to international endeavours towards these objectives. Many international analysts also applaud Pakistan's regional denuclearization approach. Christoph Bertram argued, 'As the South Asian experience once again demonstrates, however, the main push to go nuclear lies in regional competition and conflict. Global arms restraint will, therefore, only be effective if underpinned by regional arrangements of cooperation.'[5]

India and Pakistan, have however, accepted and adopted some NCBM proposals. This illustrates that they can do business when they put their minds to it, and the conditions are permissible. In the aftermath of the Kashmir crisis of the summer of 1990, NCBMs have received serious consideration from both Indian and Pakistani scholars. The May 1998 nuclear test explosions have further reinforced the NCBM debate.

The incentive to negotiate NCBMs became significant in South Asian politics because of the recognition of parity between India and Pakistan in terms of nuclear weapons. For example, it is difficult to see how the escalation of the conflict over Kashmir (in May 1990 and during the 1999 Kargil crisis) could have been avoided were it not for the fear of nuclear escalation. Devin Hagerty notes that the past practice in South Asia indicates that in the area of crisis stability, the logic of nuclear deterrence is more robust than the logic of non-proliferation. According to him, 'The 1990 Indo-Pakistan crisis lends further support to the already impressive evidence that the chief impact of nuclear weapon is to deter war between the possessors.'[6] However, it is a debatable issue whether serious nuclear-related discussion has taken place in the region,

[5] Christoph Bertram, 'The Future of Deterrence and Non-Proliferation in the Asian Context', in Jasjit Singh, ed., *Asia's New Dawn: The Challenges to Peace and Security*, New Delhi: Knowledge World, 2000, p. 180.

[6] Devin T. Hagerty, 'Nuclear Deterrence in South Asia: The 1990 Indo-Pakistani Crisis', *International Security*, vol. 20, no. 3, Winter 1995; see also George Perkovich, 'A Nuclear Third Way in South Asia', *Foreign Policy*, no. 91, Summer 1993, p. 8. Many security analysts believe that the 1986–7 Brass Tacks exercise (conducted by India in Rajasthan) crisis was controlled due to the nuclear weapons capabilities of both India and Pakistan.

or whether it is still a desired objective. India and Pakistan have adopted and largely implemented CBM in the past. The new nuclear-related arrangements are considered important, and may prove more effective in promoting trust, while leaving the nuclear deterrence of both states unobstructed.

The genuine debate regarding NCBMs started once both sides admitted that the adversary possessed nuclear weapons capabilities and the fact that War is no longer a viable option for either state. According to Kanti Bajpai, the present programmes of CBMs between India and Pakistan go back to 1988.[7] Pakistan's nuclear programme had moved forward since the mid-1980s, and its nuclear delivery system begun to mature. These developments strengthened Pakistan's military muscle.[8] Moreover, the series of crises in the 1980s between India and Pakistan compelled both the states, and the US, to negotiate the process of NCBMs in South Asia. For instance, during the 1983–4 and 1986–7 (Exercise Brass Tacks) crises, concerns were expressed that Pakistan had developed nuclear weapons capability. Pakistan's nuclear weapons potential played a vital role in the culmination of the 1990 crisis between India and Pakistan.[9] Thus, there was a general realization that Pakistan matched India in strategic calculations.

In many aspects, the arguments that have been developed on NCBMs in South Asia during the post-May 1998 nuclear tests are dissimilar in their objectivity from those which were discussed in the pre-nuclear tests (May 1998) scenario. During that period, issues like a South Asian Nuclear Weapon Free Zone, nuclear deterrence based on nuclear ambiguity, or both states refraining from overt nuclearization, etc. were dominating the NCBM debate. In the words of Marie-France Desjardins, 'the nuclear weapon free zones are recognized worldwide as important CBMs...'.[10]

[7] Kanti Bajpai, 'CBMs: Contexts, Achievements, Functions', in Banarjee, op.cit., p. 12.

[8] Pakistan's conventional capabilities were boosted by US arms assistance, particularly F-16 fighter aircraft. In addition, after 1987, Pakistan's nuclear capability was no longer seriously in doubt.

[9] Hagerty, op. cit., n. 6 above.

[10] Marie-France Desjardins, *Rethinking Confidence Building Measures*, Adelphi Paper 307, London: Oxford University Press, Dec. 1996, p. 32.

However, the debate of late 1980 did manifest the alarmist point of view. As a result, in December 1988, both sides agreed that they should not attack each other's nuclear facilities. The agreement on non-attack of each other's nuclear installations was ratified in 1991 along with the condition of exchanging updated lists about the nuclear sites in their respective states on 1 January every year.

In the early 1990s, the issue of nuclear weapons capability dominated the NCBM debate. Nuclear weapons delivery systems did not figure prominently in that discussion. But in the following years, the short and medium nuclear-capable missiles tests by India and Pakistan added a new element to the NCBM debate. Significantly, since the May 1998 nuclear weapons explosions and the Agni and Ghauri (medium-range missiles of India and Pakistan, respectively) tests, the focus of the debate has shifted more to nuclear delivery systems, with the intention of reducing the risk of accidental, unauthorized, or ill-considered launches of nuclear weapons.

The February 1999 Lahore Agreement between India and Pakistan reflected that shift. The Lahore Agreement demonstrated that both India and Pakistan were convinced of the importance of mutually agreed CBM for improving the security environment. They agreed on some issues and decided to work together for decreasing the tension between them. During the Lahore Summit, the MoU was signed by Indian Foreign Secretary, Mr K. Raghunath and Pakistani Foreign Secretary, Mr Shamshad Ahmad. According to the MoU, both India and Pakistan had approved CBM for improving their security environment. Seven of the eight points listed in the MoU directly addressed nuclear reduction for the first time. The issues decided upon were as follows:

1. The two sides shall engage in bilateral consultations on security concepts, and nuclear doctrines, with a view to developing measures for confidence-building in the nuclear and conventional fields, aimed at avoidance of conflict.
2. The two sides would undertake to provide each other with advance notification in respect of ballistic missile flight tests, and shall conclude a bilateral agreement in this regard.

3. The sides are fully committed to undertaking national measures to reduce the risks of accidental or unauthorized use of nuclear weapons under their respective control. The two sides further undertake to notify each other immediately in the event of any accidental, unauthorized, or unexplained incident that could create the risk of fallout with adverse consequences for both sides, or an outbreak of a nuclear war between the two countries, as well as to adopt measures aimed at diminishing the possibility of such actions, or such incidents being misinterpreted by the other. The two sides shall identify/establish an appropriate communication mechanism for this purpose.
4. The two sides shall continue to abide by their respective unilateral moratorium on conducting further nuclear test explosions unless either side, in exercise of its national sovereignty, decides that extraordinary events have jeopardized its supreme interests.
5. The two sides shall conclude an agreement on prevention of incidents at sea in order to ensure the safety of navigation by naval vessels, and aircraft belonging to the two sides.
6. The two sides shall periodically review the implementation of existing CBMs, and, where necessary, set up an appropriate consultative mechanism to monitor and ensure effective implementation of these CBMs.
7. The two sides shall undertake a review of the existing communication links (e.g. between the respective Directors General, Military Operations), with a view to upgrading and improving these links, and to provide for fail-safe and secure communications.
8. The two sides shall engage in bilateral consultations on security, disarmament and non-proliferation issues within the context of negotiations on these issues in multilateral fora.[11]

[11] 'Text of Document Signed at Lahore', *Dawn*, 22 Feb. 1999. Text of the Lahore Declaration, 21 Feb. 1999, http://www.ipcs.org/documents/1999/1-jan-mar.htm; see also Chris Gagne, 'Nuclear Risk Reduction in South Asia: Building on Common Ground', in Michael Krepon and Chris Gagne, eds., *The Stability-Instability Paradox: Nuclear Weapons and Brinkmanship in South Asia*, Report no. 38, Washington, D.C.: Henry L. Stimson Center, June 2001, p. 52.

The technical details of these measures were to be worked out by experts of the two sides before mid-1999, with a view to reaching bilateral agreements. However, it never moved beyond the signing ceremony. In fact, the Kargil conflict undermined the process of NCBMs which was initiated after the May 1998 nuclear weapon tests. Significantly, the MoU signed in Lahore was the result of the nine-month-long parallel diplomatic dialogue facilitated by the US which brought the two sides to the negotiating table. The US initiative primarily was to encourage India and Pakistan into taking five steps to help avoid a destabilizing nuclear and missile competition, reduce regional tension, and bolster global non-proliferation. The main point of the Talbott Mission were broadly:

1. Declaring a voluntary moratorium on further testing.
2. Refraining from producing more fissile material.
3. Observing a restraint in the development and deployment of missiles and aircraft capable of carrying WMD.
4. Tightening export control on sensitive material and technology.
5. Engaging in a direct, high-level, frequent, and, above all, productive dialogue.

Foreign Secretaries Mr Shamshad Ahmed Khan and Mr K. Raghunath met in October 1998 to formally discuss two outstanding issues: peace, security, and CBM; and Jammu and Kashmir. Despite the continued impasse over Kashmir, each side came to the table with a list of proposals for avoiding dangerous conflicts.[12] Notably, the texts of the proposals exchanged by the foreign secretaries of India and Pakistan in October 1998 have not been made public. However, in his article 'Nuclear Risk Reduction in South Asia: Building on Common Ground', Chris Gagne paraphrased the information about those proposals, which he gathered from anonymous officials' interviews.

[12] Ibid., p. 49.

According to Gagne, the Indian proposals included the following:[13]

1. Agree to an NFU pact. India had made this offer repeatedly since July 1998. New Delhi reiterated its unilateral commitment to NFU in a proposal entitled 'Preventive Use of Nuclear Weapons', which asserted that nuclear weapons should never be used. It proposed that both India and Pakistan develop an agreement on preventing nuclear war due to accidental or unauthorized use of nuclear weapons.
2. Formalize an agreement on advanced notification of ballistic missile flight tests. India also suggested that any such tests should not be conducted in the direction of the other party. The proposal suggested that notification of ballistic missile tests above a certain threshold would lead to greater transparency and predictability.
3. Extend the Agreement on Prohibition of Attack against Nuclear Installations and Facilities to include a promise not to target population and economic centres with nuclear weapons.
4. Verify and exchange seismic data. Such an exchange would assuage fears that either country was secretly conducting further tests. The exchange of information would be conducted with a view to enhancing cooperation and transparency and would also help scientists develop a better understanding of regional seismic characteristics.
5. Cooperate in multilateral forums towards complete nuclear disarmament.
6. Improve CBM that have been agreed to but not satisfactorily implemented. Specifically, India asserted that improved communications between India and Pakistan are an important component of confidence building. In light of this, India proposed that the hotline between the Directors General of Military Operations be made fail-safe and secure with voice, fax, and computer communication. India proposed similar communi-

[13] Ibid., pp. 49–50.

cation links for the Foreign Secretaries, Chiefs of Naval Staff (Operations), Chiefs of Air Staff (Operations), and Division Commanders.

7. Enhance the Agreement on Advance Notice on Military Exercises, Manoeuvres and Troop Movements and the Agreement on Prevention of Air Space Violations and for Permitting Over Flights and Landings by Military Aircraft. India acknowledged that both agreements provide for information exchange and lead to greater transparency and predictability. Arguing that the effectiveness of the agreements needed to be enhanced, India suggested that the two countries establish a consultative working mechanism to periodically review the implementation of the agreements and explore refinements, particularly along the LOC.
8. Participate in high-level defence officer exchanges.
9. Implement a ceasefire along the LOC.
10. Cease hostile propaganda.

According to Chris Gagne, at the October 1998 meeting Pakistan presented a broad outline of proposals under the heading of 'Peace and Security' on which they elaborated.[14]

1. *Abide by the non-use of force and the peaceful settlement of disputes.* This proposal included the identification of issues of peace and security between India and Pakistan, mechanisms for the peaceful settlement of disputes, and a non-aggression pact.
2. *Implement a strategic restraint regime in South Asia including both nuclear and conventional measures.* Proposals for nuclear restraint and stabilization included the prevention of a nuclear and ballistic missile race, risk reduction mechanisms, the avoidance of nuclear conflict, a formalized moratorium on nuclear testing, the non-induction of ABM and submarine-launched ballistic missile systems, and a nuclear doctrine of minimum deterrence. As a measure for conventional restraint and stabilization, Pakistan proposed a mutual and balanced reduction of forces and armaments.
3. *Implement CBM.* Among these measures was a proposal to review existing CBMs, including measures to prevent the

[14] Ibid.

> violation of airspace and territorial waters, and the prior notification of military exercises. Pakistan also proposed to enhance and upgrade the existing hotlines between the DGMOs and sector commanders as well as the hotline between the Prime Ministers. Other measures included a revival of pre-Simla ground border rules and restraint on hostile propaganda.

Many security analysts are agreed that the dialogue process between the two countries should be revived, and other measures in the MoU pursued. Though India and Pakistan had expressed differences on how to reduce the risk of conflict, they also found significant common ground.

There is a realization in India and Pakistan that deterrence based on MAD is not a pragmatic defensive strategy. Consequently, their strategic analysts condemned this strategy and termed it very dangerous for durable regional peace and security. They consider NCBMs fundamental for the security of both states. Lt. Gen. Talat Masood (retd), a Pakistani security analyst, held the view that in the face of the enormous and significant dangers of nuclear conflict, there is an urgent need to develop comprehensive CBMs. It would be a fallacy to believe that there is an advantage in keeping the nuclear danger alive so as to force a recalcitrant India to the negotiating table.[15]

P. R. Chari, an Indian security analyst, argued that an agreement on prevention of incidents at sea, setting up appropriate consultative mechanisms to monitor and ensure effective implementation of these (negotiated) CBMs, and engaging in bilateral consultations on security, disarmament and non-proliferation issues ought to be concluded. 'In my view, the most urgent item on the agenda is their engagement in bilateral consultations on security, disarmament and non-proliferation issues to negotiate confidence-building measures aimed at avoiding conflict', he stated[16]

[15] Talat Masood, 'Confidence-Building Measures: Concepts and Application', in Ahmar, ed., *The Challenge of Confidence-Building in South Asia*, New Delhi: Har-Anand Publications, 2001, p. 30.

[16] P.R. Chari, 'Nuclear Restraint, Nuclear Risk Reduction, and the Security-Insecurity Paradox in South Asia' in Krepon and Gagne, op. cit., n. 11 above, p. 32.

CHAPTER 7

American and Russian Nuclear Preventive Pursuits

If the European nations could live with eyeball-to-eyeball confrontation between the NATO and Warsaw Pact forces for decades, why should a grim view be taken of the nuclear build-up by India and Pakistan? Is Cold War brinkmanship a model for diplomacy between India and Pakistan? The case of the US and the Soviet Union is less demanding than the case of India and Pakistan, which have a common border. A missile launched from the continental US would have taken about 30 minutes to reach Russia. Further, the US and Russia spent untold billions of dollars on setting up elaborate early warning systems comprising satellites, radar systems, high-speed reliable communication links and so on, to detect and follow missile and rocket launches.[1] Nuclear risk reduction during the Cold War was a high priority and a constant preoccupation of both Soviet and American leaders. Despite that both sides experienced several close calls and barely avoided potentially catastrophic accidents.[2]

India and Pakistan do not need to subject themselves indefinitely to the tensions, uncertainties and worries of the type experienced by some European nations during the Cold War. Do they have a choice? Both India and Pakistan—whatever be the reasons—have deliberately opted to develope nuclear weapons and

[1] M.V. Ramana, 'Op-Ed: Missiles and Fast Delivery of Nuclear Destruction', *Daily Times*, 16 May 2002, http://www.dailytimes.com.pk/default.asp?page=story_16-5-2002_pg3_2

[2] Michael Krepon, 'Nuclear Risk Reduction: Is Cold War Experience Applicable to Southern Asia?', in Krepon and Gagne, eds., *The Stability-Instability Paradox: Nuclear Weapons and Brinkmanship in South Asia*, Report no. 38, Washington, D.C.: Henry L. Stimson Center, June 2001, p. 1.

missile capabilities. Significantly, despite their adversarial stances, the US and former Soviet Union had established contacts at various levels, and in some cases, agreed to a set of do's and don'ts to keep the situation manageable. There are no such agreements between India and Pakistan at the moment. The absence of dialogue between India and Pakistan increases the chances of use of nuclear weapons owing to miscalculations. The Cold War East-West model centainly does not control the nuclear risks in South Asia. It might be useful to consider the key elements of nuclear risk reduction mechanisms developed elsewhere and learn from past experiences, and mistakes. Scientific data on the security of nuclear devices and warheads is essential for avoiding nuclear accidents.

During the Cold War, the common interests of the superpowers to avoid nuclear conflict were strong enough to moderate hostile behaviour and create, through dialogue and CBM, some level of trust. Important nuclear risk reduction-related steps between nuclear powers date back to the joint US–USSR initiatives of the early 1970s. These applied to three areas: limitation and elimination of military missile inventory, missile launch transparency measures, and the prevention of proliferation of missile nuclear weapons. Specifically, these bilateral initiatives led to the 1972 ABM Treaty, followed by the Treaty on the Elimination of Intermediate-Range and Shorter Range Missiles (ground-launched missiles with a range of 500 to 5,500 km.) and START I and START II Treaties providing for significant missile and warhead reductions. In addition, launch transparency measures have been dealt with, among other things, in an Agreement on Measures to Reduce the Risk of Outbreak of Nuclear War (1971), Agreement on the Prevention of Incidents On and Over the High Seas (1972), Agreement on Notifications of Launches of Intercontinental Ballistic Missiles and Submarine-Launched Ballistic Missiles (1988), Agreement on the Establishment of Nuclear Risk Reduction Centres (1987).

The US and the Russian Federation took steps to maintain stability in the nuclear relationship in the months and years immediately following the Soviet Union's collapse. This was accomplished successfully through a cooperative effort of those involved in policy-making, and science and technology on both sides in a programme known by various names: Nunn-Lugar, Safe and Secure Reductions and finally Cooperative Threat Reduction.[3] Both sides agreed on a number of individual initiatives like accident response equipment; rail car upgrade; nuclear materials containers; nuclear material storage facility; transport vehicles; and accounting and control[4] under the Cooperative Threat Reduction programme. Neither party perceived any of these initiatives as compromising national security interests. This discussion reveals that some of the nuclear risk avoiding measures that the Americans and Russians opted for during the Cold War and in the post-Cold War period could be used as guidelines in the Indo-Pakistan adversarial scenario.

[3] William J. Burns, 'The Nuclear Issue: Nuclear Weapons, the United States, and Pakistan', *Pak–US Strategic Dialogue*, IPRI Paper no. RP 3/02, May 2002, p. 23.

[4] For the details of these initiatives, see ibid., pp. 24, 25.

CHAPTER 8

Nuclear Risk Reduction Measures

There is no agreed nuclear risk reduction framework between India and Pakistan. Although India has pledged an NFU policy, that policy would lose much of its relevance if it went down the nuclear road, since Pakistan would have to respond to capabilities rather than declared intention. For example, it would be hard for Pakistan to take at face value a declared Indian second-strike capability, as it could also be used for a decapitating first strike.[1] Moreover, among its other recommendations, the National Security Advisory Board had asked the Indian government to review its NFU of nuclear weapons policy in light of the history of the last four years in its *National Security Review*, submitted to National Security Adviser, Brajesh Mishra, in December 2002.[2] The CCS did not accept the recommendation for opting for the first-use option of nuclear weapons, but it revised its NFU policy by including the option to consider the use of nuclear weapons in case India or its Armed Forces are subjected to chemical or biological weapons attack. To be precise, it makes sense that a country with large conventional resources will not renounce the option of NFU using nuclear weapons. Nevertheless, it does generate the impression that the Indians could alter their NFU.

Moreover, India's NFU proposal is not acceptable for Pakistan because the option of first use of nuclear weapons is based on the assumption that conventional weapons can be as destructive as nuclear weapons. Second, aggression with superior conventional force requires asymmetrical war fighting strategies. Therefore, retaliation against a superior Indian conventional force attack

[1] Nazir Kamal, *Pakistani Perceptions and Prospects of Reducing the Nuclear Danger in South Asia*, Cooperative Monitoring Center Occasional Paper, US: Sandia National Laboratories, Jan. 1999.

[2] 'Abandon No-First-Use Policy, Security Board Tells Govt.', 9 Jan. 2003, http://www.rediff.com/news/2003/jan/09ia.htm

compels Pakistan to use its nuclear capabilities for its defence. This lesson has been learned from the NATO experience. NATO adopted a strategy permitting the first use of nuclear weapons to counter what then was seen as superior Soviet conventional forces. Similarly, as (nowadays) Russia no longer held superiority in conventional Armed Forces over NATO, it dropped its NFU policy, to deter a conventional war.[3]

Many Pakistani strategists, therefore, believe that Pakistan should not compromise on its option of first use of nuclear weapons. The conventional arms gap between Pakistan and India is significantly wide, and is expected to grow even wider. The scenario has become more complex after Indian Defence Minister George Fernandes' statement on 5 January 2000 that Pakistan's possession of nuclear weapons does not rule out the possibility of a limited conventional war.[4]

They believe that the nuclear weapons capability of Pakistan is the equalizing factor in the existing arms imbalance between the two neighbours. Adopting an NFU policy has the effect that conventional war can be fought between India and Pakistan that will probably not involve nuclear weapons. It would not only encourage, but also strengthen the argument of the Indian strategic analysts, who believe in achieving certain objectives by limited conventional war. Pakistan's nuclear weapons are to deter conventional as well as nuclear aggression against it. Thus, it seems impossible that Pakistan will choose an NFU option in its nuclear posture, in the near future.

The absence of dialogue, and the 2002 confrontation between India and Pakistan have further complicated and jeopardized the situation. Moreover, the possibility of the use of nuclear weapons in the region because of accident, miscalculation, or unauthorized use has increased tremendously. Concerted action by both India and Pakistan is the only way to reduce nuclear dangers in the region.

[3] Nikolai Sokov, 'Russia's Approach to Nuclear Weapons', *The Washington Quarterly*, vol. 20, no. 3, Summer 1997, pp. 107–14. See also Michael Quinlan, 'The Development of NATO Nuclear Doctrine', *Journal of the United Service Institution of India*, vol. CXXX, no. 540, Apr.–June 2000, pp. 285–6.

[4] Afzal Mahmood, 'India's Aggressive Posture', *Dawn*, 31 Jan. 2000.

The following are some important measures for nuclear risk reduction in the region.

RESOLVING THE KASHMIR ISSUE

Kashmir is the most longstanding and a crimonious dispute between Pakistan and India. Both countries have dominant interests in Kashmir. They have rigid and contradicting approaches regarding the solution of the Kashmir problem. Unless there is flexibility in the official stances of both states, the solution is impossible. Both India and Pakistan have to acknowledge the fact that war between India and Pakistan is not a solution for the Kashmir dispute. President Musharraf had categorically stated in the Agra 2001 Summit, and repeated afterward (at many occasions), that dialogue over the issue between the parties is a pragmatic approach for resolution of the dispute.

Significantly, the present environment is quite different from 1948. The concepts and approaches that were operative in the late 1940s mean little in the current scenario. Therefore, the Kashmir dispute requires innovative approaches if it is to be resolved. New ground realities must be taken into account to develop new models for solution. Continuing with past policies and insecuraities may cause a further deterioration in relations between India and Pakistan.

The settlement of the Kashmir dispute will, certainly, dramatically lower the tension between India and Pakistan. It would have a positive impact on the implementation of bilateral agreements between India and Pakistan. Consequently, both states would be in a better situation to cap, reverse, and finally eliminate their nuclear weapons programmes. President Pervez Musharraf expressed a similar desire: In response to a question during an interview broadcast on 4 May 2003 night on ARY television channel, when he said if the Kashmir dispute was resolved and there was peace and security in the region, 'South Asia could be denuclearised mutually by India and Pakistan.'[5]

[5] 'Musharraf Links Nuke-Free S. Asia to Kashmir Solution', *Daily Times*, 5 May 2003.

INDIAN AND PAKISTANI NUCLEAR DOCTRINES: DECLARATION

On 17 August 1999, an officially constituted advisory panel to the Indian National Security Council released India's draft Nuclear Doctrine.[6] Significantly, the approval of the Indian Parliament is still awaited. Pakistan's nuclear doctrine has yet to be announced. Even though, some of the salient features of the nuclear doctrines are known these do not serve the real purpose of understanding the nuclear policy of the two States. They are not enough to promote sustainable and durable nuclear stability in the region. Therefore, it is imperative that both India and Pakistan make clearer declarations, linking their doctrines to realistic and rational strategic objectives.

IMPROVEMENT OF COMMAND AND CONTROL ARRANGEMENTS

Dr Shaun Gregory defined command and control structure as 'an arrangement of facilities, personnel, procedures and means of information acquisition, processing, dissemination and decision-making used by national command authorities and military commanders in planning, directing and controlling military operations'.[7] This means that command and control is about decision-making, the exercise of direction by a properly designated commander over assigned and attached forces in the accomplishment of a mission, and is supported by information technology (IT, or the computers and communication part of C4I).[8]

[6] Text of the Draft Report of the National Security Advisory Board on Indian Nuclear Doctrine, announced on 17 Aug. 1999, New Delhi: Government of India, 17 Aug. 1999.

[7] Shaun R. Gregory, *Nuclear Command and Control in NATO: Nuclear Weapons Operations and Strategy of Flexible Response*, London: Macmillan Press, 1996, pp. 3–4.

[8] The acronym C4I stands for 'Command, Control, Communications, Computers, and Intelligence' See *Realizing The Potential of C4I Fundamental Challenges*, Washington, D.C.: National Academy Press, 1999, pp. 28, 29, 30.

Rapid developments in the field of IT and the expectation that C4I technology can dramatically increase force effectiveness have made this technology a critical element of military modernization. India and Pakistan have limited access to advanced computing and communication technology, which undermines the reliability of their C4I capabilities. The problem has become even more challenging with the development of nuclear-capable ballistic and cruise missiles.

Engaging targets that are mobile or relocatable or that have short dwell times is another challenging task that could be improved through rapid assessment of target changes and feedback to the attacking units. Rapid progress in information and communications technologies dramatically enhances the strategic role of information; positioning effective exploitation of these technological advances as a critical success factor in military affairs. These technological advances are drivers and enablers for the 'nervous system' of the military, its C4I system, to more effectively use the 'muscle' side of the military, namely the weapons platforms and troops.

Significantly, the more military leverage that C4I systems provide for the forces, the larger the incentives are for an opponent to attack those systems. Indeed, it makes little sense for an opponent to challenge symmetrically, i.e. force on force. More likely avenues of challenge are asymmetric ones that exploit potential vulnerabilities. Attacking C4I systems, whether directly or indirectly, is only one of many possible asymmetric attacks. It entails that C4I systems must be guarded properly.

In addition to sophisticated computer and communication technologies, well-trained C4I professionals are essential to the successful operation of modern military weapons such as jet fighters, warships, and sophisticated ground-based missiles. C4I professionals not only enhance the potential of fighting forces, they are significant for avoiding unauthorized use of nuclear weapons.

Indian and Pakistani military plans, however, are not creating either the environment or the incentives to attract and educate such human resources. One problem is that they have not yet found a way to integrate their C4I personnel into combat line elements, and to make them fully conversant with military doctrine, strategy, and tactics. On the other hand they are often regarded as implementers of high-level strategy decisions that are made without their input.[9]

In the nuclear context, a safe and reliable command and control system is the centrepiece in a design of stable deterrence. It is because command and control systems are developed by states to ensure that nuclear weapons are used only when authorized by the legitimate decision-makers, and their unauthorized and accidental use is entirely ruled out. Therefore, it seems appropriate that India and Pakistan take into consideration the following recommendations for overcoming the nuclear command- and control-related risks:

1. Senior commanders of both India and Pakistan must have a good understanding of how best to exploit C4I to enhance military operations.
2. The C4I specialists must be trained in the doctrine, strategy, tactics, and combat employment of military forces and be fully integrated into combat units and operational planning elements of the military forces.
3. In order to explore and develop new ideas for the use of IT to support military needs, the concerned governments should establish institutes for military IT. The aim of the proposed institutes would be to facilitate intellectual risk taking by bringing together combat operators, military information technologists, and civilian IT experts from academia and industry for extended periods of time in an environment where innovative ideas for using IT to support military needs could be explored relatively freely. They would learn how C4I technology could be used effectively to improve military effectiveness.
4. The increasing reliance on C4I systems and an increased use of commercial technologies to build these systems has brought a new and increased set of risks associated with the vulnerability of these systems to attack. There is need for good

[9] Ibid., p. 21.

automated tools for checking and inspecting network and system configurations, and tools that allow the rapid and high-confidence identification of a cyber-attacker and retaliation against such attackers. A distinction must be maintained between attackers whose intent is to disrupt or corrupt C4I systems, and one whose intent is to monitor and collect information from one.[10] So the reaction should be appropriate.

5. The C4I systems must be secured against opponents' attacks. Integrated C4I systems which exchange data and work together help military forces to prevail against adversaries by operating in a rapid, coherent, and coordinated fashion. Commanders at all levels can control their forces and apply their weapons with a high degree of precision, certainty of location, and awareness of the environment and of enemy actions and intentions. Responsive and reliable IT provides timely intelligence, greater situational awareness, and a single integrated operational picture of the battlefield. Therefore, C4I systems must be secured against opponents' attacks.

INCREASE OF STRATEGIC WARNING TIME

'Strategic Warning Time' denotes the time interval between the emergence of a nuclear threat and one's ability to respond to it. So far, the world has sought to bring it as close to zero as possible. In the India-Pakistan case, we need to fix it to a reasonable interval, say 40 minutes, so that a potentially disastrous situation can be defused through dialogue. For that, time is essential. This solution will imply putting a physical distance between the delivery vehicle and the warhead.[11] Both states would place de-alerted warheads in storage sites at some distance from their launch vehicles. They would also allow placing neutral observers at those sites, with authority only to count what went in and what went out.

[10] Ibid., p. 63.

[11] Shaukat Qadir, 'Op-Ed: Nuclear South Asia: Reducing Risks', *Daily Times*, 11 May 2002, http://www.dailytimes.com.pk/default.asp?date=5/11/02

NON-DEPLOYMENT OF NUCLEAR WEAPONS

The non-weaponized deterrence regime between India and Pakistan was transformed into a weaponized regime after their nuclear tests and both states' policies of weaponization. India and Pakistan have also commissioned their short- and intermediate-range nuclear-capable ballistic missiles with their Armed Forces. The deployment of ballistic missiles poses severe consequential security risks given the relatively short distances between major population centres in India and Pakistan, and the brief time required for missiles to travel such distances.[12]

The deployment of nuclear weapons compresses decision-making cycles for national leaders and battlefield commanders, reducing stability during times of crisis. Operational capabilities also can create a hair-trigger situation that would put the South Asian populace under acute psychological strain. Moreover, in an era of potential nuclear terrorism, the theft of a nuclear weapon from a storage site could spell an eventual disaster for a city, but the capture of a strategic missile or group of missiles ready for immediate firing could be apocalyptic for entire nations.[13]

Therefore, non-deployment of nuclear weapons by India and Pakistan would be an effective strategy to avoid one of the biggest terrorist threats, which stems largely from the extremely high launch-readiness of tactical and strategic missiles. To be precise, it is critical that India and Pakistan reduce build-up of operational capabilities to avoid going further down the nuclear road.[14]

[12] Pakistan's geographical narrowness or lack of strategic depth and the Indians' commitment to introducing more sophisticated nuclear-capable delivery systems, like cruise missiles and ballistic missile defence systems undermine Pakistan's security, and, consequently, limit its choices during crisis.

[13] Bruce G. Blair, 'The New Nuclear Threat', *Daily Times*, 5 May 2003.

[14] India's declared China-specific nuclear deterrent compels it to deploy nuclear-capable missiles or operationalize its nuclear capabilities. But many analysts, for example Nazir Kamal, believe that 'India does not need to nuclearize against China. China has an NFU policy and a conventional conflict between them, as in the past, is most likely to be limited in scope, both geographically and politically. They are also well-matched along the Himalayan frontiers. Furthermore, the danger of conflict between them is much lower than between India and Pakistan, as they

NUCLEAR RISK REDUCTION CENTRES

Communication systems form a necessary backbone for threat-reduction and monitoring. Kent L. Biringer argued that 'the process of managing missile possession in tense regions demands a reliable, secure, dedicated, and timely communications infrastructure'.[15] India and Pakistan could establish Nuclear Risk Reduction Centres (NRRCs) in their capitals and a special facsimile communications link between these centres. Michael Krepon wrote, '[a] key element in Cold War nuclear risk reduction was the establishment of reliable lines of communication across borders, for both political and military leaders'.[16] The centres are intended to supplement existing means of communication and provide direct, reliable, high-speed systems for the transmission of notifications and communications at the government-to-government level.

The centres would communicate by direct satellite links that could rapidly transmit full texts and graphics. In addition, NRRCs could be manned by mixed groups of officials from both sides to defuse crises before they erupted. In this respect, the centres would have a communications capability very similar to—but separate from—the modernized 'hot line', normally reserved for heads of government.

The NRRCs would serve an effective, exclusive and dedicated technical means of official communication for exchanging rapid, accurate, and factual information. This could help prevent misperception or unintended reactions that could lead to accidental or inadvertent escalation. The second element of NRRCs may be a verification mechanism, which could prove essential in building trust. It may include observers or inspectors to physically verify the authenticity of intelligence when there is doubt. Certainly, it

---

have moved toward a significant reduction of border tension over the past decade.' See Kamal, op. cit., n. 1 above.

[15] Kent L. Biringer, 'Missile Threat Reduction and Monitoring in South Asia', in Krepon and Gagne, eds., *The Stability-Instability Paradox: Nuclear Weapons and Brinkmanship in South Asia*, Report no. 38, Washington, D.C.: Henry L. Stimson Center, June 2001, p. 68.

[16] Krepon and Gagne, eds., ibid., p. 6.

could set a positive precedent by incorporating transparency and verification measures into military procedures. Consequently, it could serve to build trust and confidence between the two sides.[17]

RESPECT FOR SOVEREIGN EQUALITY AND TERRITORIAL INTEGRITY

The first key element in the US–Soviet context for avoiding nuclear war was a formal agreement not to change the territorial status quo in sensitive areas by military means. The tacit agreement not to seek territorial changes by force of arms was formalized in the Helsinki 'Final Act' in 1975.

The guiding principles of the Helsinki accord were: respect for sovereign equality and territorial integrity of participating states; rejection of force or threat to use force; and the inviolability of frontiers.[18] In the case of India and Pakistan, developing an understanding that both states should respect each other's sovereign equality and integrity is essential. Otherwise, issues such as Siachen Glacier and Kargil prolong deployment at the border, which might lead to an all-out war ending in nuclear devastation.

Respect for sovereign equality and territorial integrity could lead to new thoughts on resolving antagonism. However, the unresolved Kashmir issue continues to keep the risks of a nuclear conflict at a high level. The resolution of the Kashmir issue will have to come from options that preclude a military solution. Since an all out war is certainly not an option. A formal agreement not to change territorial status quo areas by military means is therefore essential and a step in the right direction.

PERSONNEL RELIABILITY PROGRAMME (PRP)

Nuclear weapons are vulnerable to loss, theft, sabotage, unauthorized use, unauthorized destruction, unauthorized disablement,

[17] Col. Rafi-uz Zaman Khan, *Pakistan and India: Can NRRCs Help Strengthen Peace?*, Occasional Paper no. 49, Washington, D.C.: Henry L. Stimson Center, Dec. 2002, http://www.stimson.org/southasia/pdf/nrrcsouthasia.pdf

[18] Krepon and Gagne, eds., op. cit., n. 15 above, pp. 1–2.

jettisoning, or accidental damage and therefore, only those personnel who qualify a Personnel Reliability Programme (PRP) should be allowed to perform duties associated with nuclear weapons, and these must be continuously evaluated for adherence to PRP standards. In addition, procedural controls, such as the two-man rule (no single employee being left alone in a sensitive area), decrease the chances of nuclear mishaps. Scott D. Sagan wrote that 'individual military officers certainly have become mentally unstable; but psychological testing under the military's PRP and the two-man rule system (under which two people are required to be involved in all nuclear weapons operations) are designed to ensure that no unstable individual could ever gain control of a US nuclear weapons'.[19] The important qualification standards of PRP are the following:

1. Physical competence, mental alertness, and technical proficiency commensurate with duty requirements.
2. Evidence of dependability in accepting responsibilities and effectively performing in an approved manner; flexibility in adjusting to changes in the working environment.
3. Evidence of good social adjustment, emotional stability, and ability to exercise sound judgement in meeting adverse or emergency situations.
4. A positive attitude towards nuclear weapon duty.

Any of the following traits or conduct should be grounds for the disqualification or decertification of individuals from PRP standards.

1. Alcohol abuse: individual(s) diagnosed as alcohol-dependent.
2. Drug abuse.
3. Any individual found to have been involved in the unauthorized trafficking, cultivating, processing, manufacturing, or sale of any narcotic or dangerous drug, shall render an individual ineligible for PRP duties.

[19] Scott D. Sagan, *The Limits of Safety: Organizations, Accidents, and Nuclear Weapons*, Princeton: Princeton University Press, 1993, p. 250.

It is significant that the armed forces of both states employ a rigorous clearance procedure and officers who are appointed to sensitive posts require additional medical clearance to prove that they have no psychiatric problems. These procedures remove the risk of unstable civilian or military officers getting control of a nuclear weapon. However, Western analysts have expressed reservations about the PRP arrangements in India and Pakistan. It is important therefore that India and Pakistan improve their PRP standards by rectifying the drawbacks which had been pointed out by neutral observers.

Without the assistance of the employee(s) of nuclear facilities, theft of nuclear material from the facilities is very difficult. Nuclear trafficking in the former Soviet Union reveals the involvement of employees in theft cases. In 1992, for example, an employee of the facility stole approximately 1.5 kg. of HEU from the Luch Scientific Production Association in Podolsk, Russia.[20] William C. Potter and Elena Sokova wrote:,'sources of material for the ten cases in 1992–95 varied from nuclear submarines fuel storage sites to research institutes to fuel fabrications facilities. In the majority of cases, the material was stolen by an employee of the facility acting alone and motivated by dire economic circumstances.'[21]

New Delhi and Islamabad must take precautionary measures to avoid or disrupt the nexus between employees of nuclear facilities/research institutes and organized criminal groups which are more inclined today to accept the risk of nuclear trafficking because of the promise of financial gain.

TRANSPARENCY MECHANISM: MAINTENANCE OF DATA

India and Pakistan should maintain a nuclear weapons register in addition to the one maintained by IAEA. The nuclear weapons register maintains the following data/information.

[20] William C. Potter and Elena Sokova, 'Illicit Nuclear Trafficking in the NIS: What's New? What's True?', *The Nonproliferation Review*, vol. 9, no. 2, Summer 2002, p. 113.

[21] Ibid.

1. Weapons holdings.
2. Nuclear weapons storage sites and facilities.
3. Military stocks of fissile material.

These data would be used for extending bilateral transparency and confidence building mechanisms related to nuclear weapons and fissile material holdings between India and Pakistan.

ESTABLISHING TRAINED UNITS TO DEAL WITH NUCLEAR SMUGGLING

Theft and smuggling of nuclear weapons or their essential ingredients by terrorist organizations is a constant risk. Well-organized terrorist groups could potentially make at least a crude nuclear bomb if they could get enough of the necessary Plutonium or HEU. The amount of material needed for a bomb is small—4 kg. of Plutonium, an amount smaller than that in a soda can—and about three times that amount of HEU is potentially enough for a nuclear weapon.[22]

Both India and Pakistan, therefore, should have at least a small unit of law enforcement officers capable of investigating nuclear smuggling cases. These officers should have the training and equipment to distinguish between, for example, intensely radioactive caesium and weapon-usable Plutonium, or between relatively innocuous low-enriched Uranium and weapon-usable HEU.[23]

CONSTRUCTIVE ROLE OF NON-NUCLEAR SOUTH ASIAN STATES

In the atmosphere of mutual mistrust and antogonism that presists between India and Pakistan there are chances of a nuclear conglagration that could lead to total destruction for much of South

[22] Matthew Bunn, 'A Detailed Analysis of Urgently Needed New Steps to Control Warheads and Fissile Material' in Joseph Cirincione, ed., *Repairing the Regime: Preventing the Spread of Weapons of Mass Destruction*, New York: Routledge, 2000, p. 74.

[23] Ibid., pp. 103, 104.

Asia. Strategic analysts are convinced that the after effects of a future total war between India and Pakistan would not be limited to the subcontinent but would have a perilous backlash for the region, in particular, and internationally, in general.

It is deplorable that, there is as yet no regional (South Asian) nuclear non-proliferation or risk-avoiding regime in place. Though India had rejected Pakistan's proposal for creating South Asia as a nuclear weapon free zone, it doesn't mean that it would oppose all regional nuclear risk avoiding initiatives. Christoph Bertram argued, 'As the South Asian experience once again demonstrates, however, the main push to go nuclear lies in regional competition and conflict. Global arms restraint will, therefore, only be effective if underpinned by regional arrangements of cooperation.'[24]

India and Pakistan may certainly accept or accommodate those regional initiatives which do not undermine their nuclear deterrence—India against China, and Pakistan against India. There are many areas where the non-NWS of South Asia could play an important role. For instance, monitoring of nuclear facilities, checking and assisting in safeguarding nuclear facilities, verification of data, nuclear CBM, etc.

The credibility and working of bilateral agreements, for example, requires a regional facilitator which can monitor and make non-biased judgements about the commitment and sincerity of both states with to bilateral agreements. The facilitator must be a group of regional states (SAARC members) whose security has been jeopardized by the overt nuclearization of India and Pakistan. In fact, they have a legitimate interest in avoiding the nuclear risks in South Asia.

Therefore, it seems appropriate that the South Asian states constitute a regional forum/regime for addressing nuclear related-risks in South Asia. Admittedly, the success of this regime de-

[24] Christoph Bertram, 'The Future of Deterrence and Non-Proliferation in the Asian Context', in Jasjit Singh, ed., *Asia's New Dawn: The Challenges to Peace and Security*, New Delhi: Knowledge World, 2000, p. 180.

pends upon the sincerity and commitment of India and Pakistan to the regime. Nevertheless, undermining the legitimate concerns of the South Asian neighbours is not an easy task for both the regional NWS.

NUCLEAR WARHEADS AND FISSILE MATERIAL: REGIONAL VERIFICATION REGIME

Agreeing on and setting up an effective regional verification regime is usually a long-term process. This process often starts with confidence-building and transparency measures that eventually evolve into a more intrusive verification regime. Specially in sensitive areas related to national security, prior experience with declaration and inspection procedures can facilitate the implementation of complex verification arrangements. A favourable precedent in this regard is that in February 1999, during the Lahore Summit, India and Pakistan agreed to promulgation of mutually agreed CBM for improving the security environment.[25]

Under the regional verification regime, both India and Pakistan will have to declare the numbers and locations of their nuclear weapons to the regime's secretariat. They will probably also be required to publish a historical account of their nuclear weapons programmes. Notably, the exchange of nuclear information between the two countries has a precedent in the agreement to annually exchange information on the location of nuclear installations as per the 1991 Agreement on the Non-Attack of Nuclear Facilities. Under this agreement, India and Pakistan are obliged to exchange lists of nuclear facilities on the first business day of each year. Thus far, nuclear facilities-related lists have been exchanged between each other. Such a 'baseline declaration' submitted by both countries would establish the basis on which the level of nuclear weapons proliferation will be monitored. This

[25] See 'Text of Document Signed at Lahore', *Dawn*, 22 Feb. 1999; Text of the Lahore Declaration, 21 Feb. 1999, http://www.ipcs.org/documents/1999/1-jan-mar.htm

objective, however, would only be achieved through the repeated process of declarations by both countries and their off-site and on-site monitoring activities.[26]

[26] Russia and the US have acquired verification experience during the implementation of the Intermediate-Range Nuclear Forces (INF), Strategic Arms Limitation Talks (SALT), and Strategic Arms Reduction Talks (START) treaties, which limit numbers and types of certain nuclear delivery vehicles and deployed nuclear warheads. Both countries have already agreed in principle on a number of additional measures that would constitute first steps in implementing transparency and CBM: Oliver Meier, *The Verification of a Nuclear Weapon Free World: Closing the Gaps*, Verification Research, Training and Information Centre, http://www.reachingcriticalwill.org/nwc/mon2oliver.html

CHAPTER 9
Nuclear Restraint Regime in South Asia

While negotiating components of NRR in South Asia, it will be appropriate that a withdrawal clause be included in the agreements/treaties that would allow both India and Pakistan to leave them on short notice by applying supreme national interest. Notably, such arrangements are made in most arms control agreements. If warranted by a change in strategic circumstances, the parties would have the right to exceed the agreement's limits with notice. This would limit constraints and maximize flexibility. Consequently, either party could exceed the limits without violating the agreement by giving the requisite notice. This mechanism could increase the trust between India and Pakistan. Let us look at some of the agreements/treaties that would constitute NRR.

SOUTH ASIAN ANTI-BALLISTIC MISSILE TREATY

Pakistan and India have already signed some nuclear- and missile-related agreements, for example, the agreement not to attack each other's nuclear facilities. Both states are honouring these agreements. Though the expectations would be modest, there are possibilities for more CBM. Pakistan and India should negotiate a South Asian Anti-Ballistic Missile (SAABM) Treaty, prohibiting nationwide defences against strategic and tactical ballistic missiles and barring the development, testing, and deployment of sea, air, space and mobile land-based ABM systems or components.

The justification for an SAABM Treaty would be the mutual recognition that India and Pakistan have already attained a strategic balance based on nuclear deterrence. Neither side could launch a nuclear attack against the other without calculating the risk of a retaliatory strike that would produce unacceptable damage. Therefore, without nationwide defences, both India and Pakistan would have the confidence that the other would not risk a nuclear attack, knowing that it would be vulnerable to a retaliatory strike.

The possibility for the constitution of an SAABM Treaty between India and Pakistan is remote because of the Chinese factor in the security calculations of India. But the encouraging factor is that China opposed the development and deployment of anti-missile systems. India always legitimized its nuclear weapons programme by linking it with China's nuclear weapons capabilities. Therefore, an SAABM Treaty is also in the interest of India.

CONVENTIONAL ARMS CONTROL

India and Pakistan have been developing and procuring conventional arms as both governments are under pressure to make large allocations for conventional force modernization and to improve the condition of their military services. Defence expenditures have increased significantly in the recent years, particularly in India. President Pervez Musharraf articulated these fears in a *Newsweek* interview. He said: 'Our Army is enough for deterrence at the moment. But the Indians are increasing their defence budget, having contracted billions of dollars of purchases from Russia and the West. If they tilt the conventional balance, we shall have to restore it.'[1]

The conventional arms race could destabilize the strategic balance between India and Pakistan. Significantly, this imbalance increases the threat perceptions of Pakistan because of India's better economy, and more spending on the build-up of its armed forces. It was because of this percieved defence disadvantage, that Pakistan developed its nuclear arsenal to deter an Indian attack. In order

[1] Quoted in Parsa Venkateshwar Rao, Jr, 'A Triumph of No Value?', *Deccan Herald*, 25 July 2002, http://www.deccanherald.com/deccanherald/July25/top.htm

to retain the option of threat to indicate nuclear war, Islamabad consistently rejected a nuclear NFU policy.[2] Dr Rifaat Hussain argued: 'The fundamental problem with India's offer of nuclear NFU is that it does not address the security dilemma that a smaller and weaker Pakistan will face at the hands of a conventional militarily-superior India after Islamabad pledges itself not to have a recourse to nuclear threats to ensure its survival.'[3] To be precise, Pakistan reliance on nuclear weapons becomes not only imminent, but also logical.

In this situation, a bilateral conventional arms control agreement could reduce Pakistan's reliance on nuclear weapons. Indian defence analyst Jasjit Singh, in his book *Nuclear India*, has pointed out:

> Public, intellectual, and official opinion in Pakistan is unanimous in the belief that possession of nuclear weapons is necessary for Pakistan's security. The basic rationale has been to seek a nuclear deterrent against India's conventional superiority. Giving up the nuclear option would leave it, in its perceptions, vulnerable to India's conventional forces.... Thus Pakistan may be expected to express a willingness to agree to conventional force reduction agreements, but it is not likely to accept any commitment that undermines its nuclear deterrence against the conventional forces of India.[4]

This proves that conventional arms control is imperative. Through a bilateral treaty/agreement on conventional arms, the nuclear danger could be reduced significantly in the region.

FORCE LIMITATION ZONE AGREEMENT

The danger of nuclear war could also be reduced through conventional stability. A force limitation zone along the border would lower armament levels in forward positions and eliminate the threat of surprise attack, thereby greatly reducing the danger of

[2] For understanding more about the nuclear use option, see Rifaat Hussain, 'Thinking about Nuclear Use and No First Use', *National Development and Security*, vol. X, no. 2, Winter 2001/2, pp. 1–13.

[3] Ibid., p. 9.

[4] Ibid., p. 8.

miscalculation.[5] Significantly, an agreement exists in the India-Pakistan context prohibiting military aircraft from flying within specified distances of the border, which is generally being observed.

BAN ON NUCLAR EXERCISES

When states conduct nuclear-related military exercises, it gives the impression that they would be making their nuclear capabilities operational. During the summer of 2001, the Indian military exercise Poorna Vijay aroused many questions among Pakistani policy-makers. In fact, the officially stated purpose of the exercise was to evaluate concepts and practice battle procedures during offensive and defensive operations on the future battlefield, with a nuclear backdrop.

Islamabad viewed the exercise as being an attempt by India to legitimize conventional war waged under a nuclear umbrella. Therefore, in July 2002, Pakistan conducted a joint forces week-long war game at its National Defence College. One of the important objectives of the war game was to enhance joint planning, and to explore ways to increase Pakistan's tactical planning capabilities, specially its nuclear deterrence. Importantly, the Strategic Plans Directorate (SPD) also participated in the nuclear-related war games.[6] This indicates that in the war game, Pakistan brought the nuclear factor into practical consideration.

The nuclear-related military exercises by India and Pakistan further endanger the regional strategic environment. These exercises not only increase the importance of nuclear weapons in the military calculations of both states, but also promote a spiral of competition that usually manifests itself in an arms race that, ultimately, leads to war. It is because these exercises increase misperceptions and mistrust. Therefore, such nuclear-related military exercises ought to be avoided. In this context, the already

[5] Nazir Kamal, *Pakistani Perceptions and Prospects of Reducing the Nuclear Danger in South Asia*, Cooperative Monitoring Center Occasional Paper, US: Sandia National Laboratories, Jan. 1999.

[6] Ayesha Siddiqa-Agha, 'War-Gaming in a Nuclear Environment', *Friday Times*, 26 July–1 Aug. 2002, http://www.thefridaytimes.com/news6a.htm

existing India-Pakistan agreement for restriction on certain military exercises should be updated.

BILATERAL TACTICAL NUCLEAR WEAPONS CONTROL AGREEMENT

The definition of 'tactical' or 'substrategic' nuclear weapons is somewhat tenuous and can include many criteria, such as range, yield, target, national ownership, delivery vehicle, and capability. In simple terms, tactical nuclear weapons have smaller explosive power and limited blast damage radius measured in hundred of metres, and that cause relatively low levels of casualties than strategic nuclear weapons. Tactical nuclear weapons are intended for 'battlefield' use against enemy forces, rather than against enemy cities or strategic nuclear forces. Tactical nuclear weapons include a broad array of devices, from so-called nuclear landmines and nuclear artillery shells to airdropped or missile-launched nuclear warheads. Their yields can be relatively low (0.1 kiloton), equal to those of the bombs dropped on Hiroshima and Nagasaki (15–20 kilotons), or very large (1 megaton).[7]

There are chances that India and Pakistan would deploy very low-yield nuclear weapons in the sub-kiloton or 1–2 kiloton range, because of their apparent utility on a battlefield, and which, in compact form, can even be fired from artillery guns. This is a valid belief because both India and Pakistan tested low-yield nuclear weapons. On 28 May 1998, for example, Pakistan conducted four tests of small-/low-yield weapons. The collective yield of these four weapons was 4–10 kiloton. India too had demonstrated a similar capability through its sub-kiloton tests in May 1998. According to Dr R. Chidambaram, India had developed tactical nuclear weapons.[8]

[7] Alistair Millar, 'The Pressing Need for Tactical Nuclear Weapons Control', *Arms Control Today*, May 2002, http://www.armscontrol.org/act/2002_05/millarmay02.asp

[8] Brahma Chellaney, 'India's Nuclear Planning, Force Structure, Doctrine and Arms Control Posture', in Digumarti Bhaskara Rao, *Nuclear Materials Issue and Concerns*, vol. 11, New Delhi: Discovery Publishing, 2001, p. 997.

It is significant that if India and Pakistan use tactical nuclear weapons in the battlefield, this has strategic implications. Pakistan's major industrial and populous cities are near its eastern border. Second, the use of tactical nuclear weapons increases the possibility of escalation. In 1962, President Kennedy said, 'The decision to use any kind of a nuclear weapon, even tactical ones, presents such a risk of getting out of control so quickly....'[9] The uncertainties associated with the employment of tactical nuclear weapons are simply too great. Therefore, use of tactical nuclear weapons by India would have strategic implications for Pakistan and vice versa. Moreover, they could lead to all-out nuclear war.

The less cumbersome tactical nuclear weapons and their trouble-free portability increases their vulnerability to theft by terrorists. Even in the hands of state militaries, tactical nuclear weapons are more susceptible to unauthorized or accidental use than strategic weapons: they are often deployed near the front line; they are far more sensitive to communication problems under crisis conditions; and they can be fired by a soldier in the field without going through the stringent safety precautions that govern the launch of strategic nuclear weapons. P.R. Chari argued that 'War-fighting requires tactical nuclear weapons which could be very destabilizing in the subcontinental scenario.'[10]

Therefore, while it is imperative that India and Pakistan negotiate a bilateral treaty for countering the tactical nuclear weapons threat, such an agreement would require intrusive monitoring and verification. The present mistrust between India and Pakistan does not ensure the practicability of such an agreement. But the dividends of an agreement between India and Pakistan disallowing the development and deployment of tactical nuclear weapons are impressive in terms of deterrence stability.

[9] Stansfield Turner, 'The Specter of Nuclear Proliferation', *Security Dialogue*, vol. 29, no. 3, New Delhi: Sage Publications, 1998, p. 296.

[10] P.R. Chari, 'Nuclear Restraint, Nuclear Risk Reduction, and the Security-Insecurity Paradox in South Asia', in Krepon and Gagne, eds., *The Stability-Instability Paradox: Nuclear Weapons and Brinkmanship in South Asia*, Report no. 38, Washington, D.C.: Henry L. Stimson Center, June 2001, p. 32.

NUCLEAR DATA EXCHANGE AGREEMENT TO REDUCE THREAT OF NUCLEAR TERRORISM

The operational pattern that terrorists employ to cause widespread destruction have changed fundamentally since the last quarter of the twentieth century. Newer trends differ from the old in at least three related dimensions: fewer incidents, greater casualties; the growth of religious terrorism; and nuclear, biological, and chemical terrorism. The emerging new trends warn of the multifold increase in lethality and ruthlessness. Keeping this in mind one of the most serious threats to regional security today would be if a small portion of India's or Pakistan's nuclear stockpile fall into the hands of organizations which have been involved in terrorist activities in South Asia.

India and Pakistan must negotiate a data exchange agreement about their respective arsenals and a comprehensive inventory of all nuclear weapons and material in both countries in order to combat the serious threat of nuclear terrorism.

COOPERATIVE MONITORING AGREEMENT FOR THE LOC

The LOC (about 740 km.) extends south of Siachen through the former princely state of Kashmir. This line was established in 1949 as a CFL at the conclusion of the first India-Pakistan war in 1948. The CFL was formalized with the signing of the Karachi Agreement in July 1949. Following the third India-Pakistan war in 1971, the CFL (with some modification) became the LOC. The Simla Agreement of July 1972 specified the LOC resulting from the December 1971 ceasefire and called for the line to be respected by both sides without prejudice to the position of either side.[11] Ironically, both sides have been violating the LOC. Firing and skirmishes between Indian and Pakistani troops are a daily fact of life at the line. These violations could cause a serious

[11] Tahir Kheli and Biringer, *Reducing Risk in South Asia: Managing India-Pakistan Tensions*, CMC Occasional Papers, US: Sandia National Laboratories, Mar. 2001, p. 12.

crisis, like the 1999 Kargil crisis which had threatened to escalate to the level of nuclear weapons use.

Preservation of the sanctity of the LOC is an important NRRM between India and Pakistan. The LOC has been subject to numerous agreements between them. Pakistan has been advocating the proper institutionalization of the UN military observers' role on both sides of the line. A bilateral cooperative monitoring agreement for the LOC, however, does not exist between India and Pakistan. The formation of a cooperative monitoring agreement will be an important step towards regional stability. It would facilitate both sides in detecting and checking illegal cross-border movements and inspections of selected military deployments along the LOC to demonstrate compliance with ceasefire or other agreements. It may be beneficial to have an agreement to place international observers (UN or SAARC) on both sides of the LOC in order to enforce strict compliance with ceasefire and to prevent infiltration along the borders.

QUALITATIVE RESTRAINT ON NUCLEAR WEAPONS

India and Pakistan face a choice between the assured dangers of proliferation, or the challenges of disarmament. The better choice is capping, progressive reduction, and complete elimination of nuclear weapons. But the international and regional environments and their security needs do not allow them to opt for this better choice. What is possible in the current scenario is that they choose the strategy of minimum nuclear deterrence keeping in view the reality of nuclear asymmetry, and refrain from developing overkill nuclear capabilities. According to P.R. Chari, 'Pakistan needs to accept the fact that India's nuclear capability has to be designed against Pakistan and China, just as India would have to accept that China's nuclear capability must configure to the US and Russia. Strict parity would be unrealistic in the light of differing security perceptions, and seeking this goal could lead to an unrestrained arms race.'[12]

[12] Ibid., pp. 32–3.

India's and Pakistan's geo-strategic environment also permits them to live with the first generation of nuclear weapons. This entails that they do not require further nuclear weapons tests. In addition, minimum nuclear deterrence also permits them to keep fissile material for nuclear weapons limited. Thus, the correct move at present in the light of the above agreements would be that both India and Pakistan either join the international movement for CTBT and FMCT, or they make similar arrangements at the regional level.[13]

BILATERAL AGREEMENT ON MONITORING SYSTEM

The bilateral agreements, of course, need a system of monitoring of nuclear storage areas and nuclear facilities. This indicates that the monitoring system involve the declaration of nuclear storage sites and facilities, and permitting monitoring teams to inspect them.

Technical monitoring of storage areas involves use of a number of sensors to detect activity level in or around the facility. Ground sensors such as seismic, magnetic, or acoustic could be used to detect movement around the facility's boundary or on access roads leading to the facility. Through these sensors, data could be collected and stored on site and sent by radio, satellite, phone, the Internet or other communication means to party/parties of the agreement.[14]

Technical monitoring of sensitive facilities involves sensors such as door switches, motion sensors, or electronic seals to detect entry or activity in the facility. The seals would indicate any incident of tampering with containers, monitoring equipment, or portions of the facility that have been closed and sealed. Moreover, the technique of use of sensor-triggered video systems which capture digital images when another sensor is activated, could be

[13] Both India and Pakistan have declared a moratorium on nuclear tests and have said that a test ban would not impinge on their security, as the tests conducted in May 1998 have given them an assured capability.

[14] Kent L. Biringer, 'Missile Threat Reduction and Monitoring in South Asia', in Krepon and Gagne, op. cit., n. 10 above, p. 73.

used to better characterize any detected interior or exterior event. The video systems are based on periodic recording of video images in nuclear facilities of interest.[15] Both India and Pakistan lack such technologies at this time, but they should develop or procure such technical equipment from the developed world.

[15] Ibid.

CHAPTER 10

Conclusion

The nuclear doctrines of both India and Pakistan are still in flux and as a consequence the possibility of certain nuclear operational-related agreements is limited. Very little is known about the true state of nuclear readiness in the two nations but the terrible shadow of nuclear weapons looms over South Asia. Realizing the perils of nuclearization, India and Pakistan agreed to exchange information on their nuclear doctrines and security concepts during the February 1999 Lahore Summit. Unfortunately the Lahore MoU has not been implemented.

India and Pakistan are in the process of developing and improving the quality of their nuclear arsenals and therefore, the scope and the level of detail about their nuclear weapons data still remains unclear.[1] The situation is further complicated by a total lack of trust between the two. One example would be the use of hot lines to convey misleading information or their disuse in crisis situations.[2]

The history of the India-Pakistan relationship reveals that traditional and recognized CBMs would be of little practical application to subcontinental peace and the resolution of the India-Pakistan dispute, because most of the agreements signed between both states in the military and non-military areas of CBMs have not been implemented. Non-implementation has

[1] Howard Diamond, 'India, Pakistan Agree on Security, Confidence-Building Measures', *Arms Control Today*, Jan/Feb 1999, http://www.armscontrol.org/act/1999_01-02/ipjf99.asp

[2] P.R. Chari, 'Nuclear Restraint, Nuclear Risk Reduction, and the Security-Insecurity Paradox in South Asia', in Krepon and Gagne, eds., *The Stability-Instability Paradox: Nuclear Weapons and Brinkmanship in South Asia*, Report no. 38, Washington, D.C.: Henry L. Stimson Center, June 2001, p. 33.

created a credibility crisis for the CBM process. While evaluating the CBM process between India and Pakistan, Dr Maleeha Lodhi stated that talks (between India and Pakistan) have often been afflicted by the joker-clause syndrome, where proposals have been made by one side with the foreknowledge that these would be unacceptable to the other. The proneness of negotiations to relapse into procedural wrangles—endless rounds of talks about talks—has prevented them from moving into serious and sustained efforts at conflict resolution.[3] Certainly, conflict resolution is a laborious task in the region due to the enormous mistrust which surrounds the India-Pakistan relationship. However, in terms of NRRMs creating effective command and control structures, maintaining a certain level of transparency, and doctrinal clarity could assist (to some extent) in overcoming the joker-clause syndrome.

India and Pakistan, however, have demonstrated reason and restraint in chalking out their nuclear policies. In the aftermath of the May 1998 nuclear explosions, both countries deferred conversion of their tested nuclear weapons into deployment, observed a moratorium on further nuclear testing, checked the nuclear weapons know-how trade, and above all, controlled the limited border war from escalation into all-out conventional war ending in a nuclear weapons exchange. It seems that outright all-out war had been ruled out because of the presence of nuclear weapons on both sides.

Stockpiles of nuclear fissile material continue to mount in India and Pakistan. The nuclear-capable missiles build-up is the preferred choice of both countries. However, they lack the experience and technology of nuclear command and control systems. In addition, a wide gap exists in the perceptions regarding nuclear weapons usage among the Indian and the Pakistani strategists. These facts pose serious threats to South Asian security. It will be extremely difficult to maintain stability and nuclear security under these extenuating circumstances. It will require a vision

[3] Maleeha Lodhi, 'Dealing with South Asia's Nuclear and Security Issues', *Defence Journal*, Jan. 1999, http://www.defencejournal.com/jan99/nuc-sec-issues.htm

and a road map of how these complex issues can be solved. Therefore, a constructive approach for containing nuclear risks in the region is imperative.

A nuclear risk reduction strategy should be founded on the principles of recognition of the existing regional and international realities regarding nuclear weapons proliferation. International discriminatory policies backed by economic sanctions against India and Pakistan have had negative consequences instead of helping to denuclearize South Asia. The Western states led by the US, in particular, pressurized both India and Pakistan that they cap, roll back, and finally eliminate their nuclear weapons capabilities.

In the international community, the Americans have been very active, adopting a carrot and stick policy against India and Pakistan. When incentives became ineffective, the US tried to apply sanctions through denial of financial aid, economic assistance, military cooperation, and access to technology. However, these sanctions endanger political relations and are frequently controversial. Sanctions against India and Pakistan did not prevent these countries from developing nuclear weapons and their delivery vehicles. It is important to note that the sanctions were lifted in the aftermath of the 11 September attack in order to secure the support of India and Pakistan in the war against terrorism in Afghanistan.

The shift in US policy from sanctions to engagement has provided an opportunity to India and Pakistan to receive assistance from the developed world in the field of nuclear know-how, specially that related to nuclear safety and security arrangements. The US and other states are in a position to guide and provide technical nuclear-related assistance to India and Pakistan. The Nunn-Lugar 'cooperative threat reduction' programme to improve the security of Russia's nuclear materials, technology, and expertise can serve as a precedent in addressing nuclear-related security problems in India and Pakistan.

In the present scenario, the leadership of both sides needs to work out ways of making a paradigm shift in relations from those based on fear and distrust to those based on trust, peace, and progress. That would require politicians on both sides to think differently and to change their basic attitude towards each other to ensure peace. In this context, a bilateral approach between India and Pakistan based on mutual trust and understanding seems a pragmatic solution to the increasing nuclear danger. A bilateral confidence building process should be supported by a regional multilateral approach.

India and Pakistan must listen to and understand the concerns of their smaller South Asian neighbours. What is in the interest of both states in particular, and South Asia in general, is that India and Pakistan start a sustainable process of dialogue to improve collaborative and unilateral actions for avoiding threat of nuclear risk.

Bibliography

Ahmar, Moonis, ed., *The Challenge of Confidence-Building in South Asia*, New Delhi: Har-Anand Publications, 2001.

———, ed., *Paradigms of Conflict Resolution in South Asia*, Dhaka: University Press, 2003.

Ahmad, Samina, 'Pakistan's Proposal for a Nuclear Weapon Free Zone in South Asia', *Pakistan Horizon*, vol. XXXII, no. 4, 1979.

Albright, David, 'The Shots Heard Around the World', *The Bulletin of Atomic Scientists*, vol. 54, no. 4, July/Aug. 1998.

Ali, Akhtar, *Pakistan's Nuclear Dilemma: Energy and Security Dimensions*, Karachi: Economic Research Unit, 1984.

Amin, Shahid M., 'Post-Nuclear South Asia—Implications, Challenges and Opportunities', *National Development and Security*, vol. VIII, no. 2, Nov. 1999.

Anthony, Ian, 'Arms Control After the Attacks of 11 September 2001', *SIPRI Yearbook 2002: Armaments, Disarmament and International Security*, London: Oxford University Press, 2002.

Arnett, Eric, 'What Threat?', *The Bulletin of Atomic Scientists*, Mar./Apr. 1997.

Azizan, Rouben, ed., *Nuclear Developments in South Asia and the Future of Global Arms Control*, Wellington: Centre for Strategic Studies, 2001.

Banerjee, Dipankar, ed., *Confidence Building Measures in South Asia*, Colombo: Regional Centre for Strategic Studies, 1999.

Barnaby, Frank, *The Role and Control of Weapons in the 1990s*, New York: Routledge, 1992.

Barash, David P., *Introduction to Peace Studies*, California: Wadsworth, 1991.

Basrur, Rajesh M., 'Nuclear India at the Crossroads', *Arms Control Today*, Sep. 2003.

Berlin, Donald L., 'Indian Ocean Redux—Arms, Bases and Re-Emergence of Strategic Rivalry', *Journal of Indian Ocean Studies*, vol. 10, no. 1, Apr. 2002.

Bidwai, Praful, 'Nuclear Chickens Come Home', *Frontline*, vol. 18, issue 23, 10–23 Nov. 2001.

Biswas, Shampa, 'Nuclear Apartheid as Political Position: Race as a

Postcolonial Resource?', *Alternatives—Global, Local, Political*, vol. 26, no. 4, Oct.–Dec. 2001.

Blank, Jonah, 'Kashmir: Fundamentalism Takes Root', *Foreign Affairs*, vol. 78, no. 6, Nov. /Dec. 1999.

Bundy, McGeorge, *Danger and Survival: Choices about the Bomb in the First Fifty Years*, New York: Random House, 1988.

Burns, William J., 'The Nuclear Issue: Nuclear Weapons, the United States, and Pakistan', *Pak–US Strategic Dialogue*, IPRI Paper no. RP 3/02, May 2002.

Cheema, Pervaiz Iqbal, *The Armed Forces of Pakistan*, Karachi: Oxford University Press, 2002.

Cirincione, Joseph, ed., *Repairing the Regime: Preventing the Spread of Weapons of Mass Destruction*, New York: Routledge, 2000.

Collina, Tom Z. and Jon B. Wolfsthal, 'Nuclear Terrorism and Warhead Control in Russia', *Arms Control Today*, Apr. 2002.

Council on Foreign Relations, *A New US Policy Towards India and Pakistan*, Report of an Independent Task Force, US: Council on Foreign Relations, 1997.

Desjardins, Marie-France, *Rethinking Confidence Building Measures*, Adelphi Paper no. 307, London: Oxford University Press, Dec. 1996.

Diamond, Howard, 'India, Pakistan Agree on Security, Confidence Building Measures', *Arms Control Today*, Jan./Feb. 1999.

Dorman, Andrew, Mike Smith, and Matthew Uttley, eds., *The Changing Face of Military Power: Joint Warfare in an Expeditionary Era*, New York: Palgrave, 2002.

Ganguly, Sumit, 'India's Pathway to Pokhran II: The Prospects and Sources of New Delhi's Nuclear Weapons Programme', *International Security*, vol. 23, no. 4, Spring 1999.

Goodpaster, Gen. J. Andress, *An Evolving US Nuclear Posture*, Washington, D.C.: Henry L. Stimson Center, 1995.

Goldblat, Jozef, 'The CTBT Negotiations', *UNIDIR Newsletter*, Special Issue, Geneva: UN, July 1997.

———, *Arms Control: The New Guide to Negotiations and Agreements*, London: Sage Publications, 2002.

Gregory, Shaun R., *Nuclear Command and Control in NATO: Nuclear Weapons Operations and Strategy of Flexible Response*, London: Macmillan Press, 1996.

Gurr, Nadine and Benjamin Cole, *The New Face of Terrorism: Threats from Weapons of Mass Destruction*, London: I.B. Tauris, 2000.

Gutteridge, William, *The New Terrorism*, London: Mansell Publishing, 1986.

Hagerty, Devin T., 'Nuclear Deterrence in South Asia: The 1990 Indo-Pakistani Crisis', *International Security*, vol. 20, no. 3, Winter 1995.

Harvey, Frank P., 'The Future of Strategic Stability and Nuclear Deterrence', *International Journal*, vol. LVIII, no. 2, Spring 2003.

Hoodbhoy, Pervez, *The Nuclear Issues Between India and Pakistan: Myths and Realities*, Occasional Paper 18, Washington, D.C.: Henry L. Stimson Center, July 1994.

Howlett, Darryl, 'The NPT Renewal Conference: Stumbling Toward 1995', *International Security*, vol. 19, no. 1, Summer 1994.

Jaspal, Zafar Nawaz, 'NPT in 2000: Challenges Ahead', *Strategic Studies*, vol. XX, no. 4, Autumn 2000.

Kak, Kapil, 'India's Conventional Defence Problems and Prospects', *Strategic Analysis*, vol. XXII, no. 11, Feb. 1999.

Kamal, Nazir, *Pakistani Perceptions and Prospects of Reducing the Nuclear Danger in South Asia*, Cooperative Monitoring Center Occasional Paper, US: Sandia National Laboratories, Jan. 1999.

Karnad, Bharat, *Nuclear Weapons and Indian Security: The Realist Foundations of Strategy*, New Delhi: Macmillan, 2002.

Khan, Col. Rafi-uz-Zaman, *Pakistan and India: Can NRRCs Help Strengthen Peace?*, Occasional Paper no. 49, Washington, D.C.: Henry L. Stimson Center, Dec. 2002.

Khan, Feroz Hassan, 'Challenges to Nuclear Stability in South Asia', *The Nonproliferation Review*, Spring 2003.

Kheli, Shirin Tahir and Kent L. Biringer, *Reducing Risk in South Asia: Managing India-Pakistan Tensions*, CMC Occasional Papers, US: Sandia National Laboratories, Mar. 2001.

Kimball, Daryl G., 'CTBT Rogue State?', *Arms Control Today*, Dec. 2001.

Kile, Shannon N., 'Nuclear Arms Control and Ballistic Missile Defense', *SIPRI Yearbook 2001: Armaments, Disarmament and International Security*, London: Oxford University Press, 2001.

Krepon, Michael and Chris Gagne, eds., *The Stability-Instability Paradox: Nuclear Weapons and Brinkmanship in South Asia*, Report no. 38, Washington, D.C.: Henry L. Stimson Center, June 2001.

Lavoy, Peter R., Scott D. Sagan, and James J. Wirtz, *Planning the Unthinkable: How New Powers Will Use Nuclear, Biological, and Chemical Weapons*, London: Cornell University Press, 2000.

Matinuddin, Lt. Gen. Kamal (retd), *Nuclear Pakistan—Impact on Geopolitical and Regional Environment*, Margalla Papers no. 2, Dec. 1998.

Mazari, Shireen M., *Nuclearization of South Asia: The Geopolitical Dimension*, Margalla Papers no. 2, Dec. 1998.

Mazari, Shireen M. and Maria Sultan, *Nuclear Safety and Terrorism: A Case Study of India*, Islamabad Papers, no. 19, 2001.

Menon, Rear Adm. Raja, *A Nuclear Strategy for India*, New Delhi: Sage Publications, 2000.

Millar, Alistair, 'The Pressing Need for Tactical Nuclear Weapons Control', *Arms Control Today*, May 2002.

Mattoo, Amitabh, ed., *India's Nuclear Deterrent: Pokhran II and Beyond*, New Delhi: Har-Anand Publications, 1999.

National Academy Press, *Realizing the Potential of C4I Fundamental Challenges*, Washington, D.C.: National Academy Press, 1999.

Nixon, Richard, *Seize the Moment: America's Challenge in a One-Superpower World*, New York: Simon & Schuster, 1992.

Perkovich, George, 'A Nuclear Third Way in South Asia', *Foreign Policy*, no. 91, Summer 1993.

———, *India's Nuclear Bomb: The Impact on Global Proliferation*, New Delhi: Oxford University Press, 2000.

———, 'Bush's Nuclear Revolution: A Regime Change in Nonproliferation', *Foreign Affairs*, Mar./Apr. 2003.

Potter, William C. and Elena Sokova, 'Illicit Nuclear Trafficking in the NIS: What's New? What's True?', *The Nonproliferation Review*, vol. 9, no. 2, Summer 2002.

Pregenzer, Arian L., 'Securing Nuclear Capabilities in India and Pakistan: Reducing the Terrorists and Proliferation Risks', *The Nonproliferation Review*, Spring 2003.

Quinlan, Michael, 'The Development of NATO Nuclear Doctrine', *Journal of the United Service Institution of India*, vol. CXXX, no. 540, Apr.–June 2000.

Rais, Rasul B., 'Pakistan in the Regional and Global Power Structure', *Asian Survey*, vol. XXXI, no. 4, Apr. 1991.

Rajen, Gaurav, 'Tactical Nuclear Weapons in South Asia: The Need to Disavow Development and Deployment', *Disarmament Forum*, UN: UNIDR, Four, 2002.

Ranger, Robin, *Arms and Politics 1958–1978: Arms Control in a Changing Political Context*, Canada: Macmillan, 1979.

Rao, Digumarti Bhaskara, *Nuclear Materials Issues and Concerns*, vol. 11, New Delhi: Discovery Publishing, 2001.

Russell, Richard L., 'The Nuclear Peace Fallacy: How Deterrence Can Fail', *The Journal of Strategic Studies*, vol. 26, no. 1, Mar. 2003.

Sagan, Scott D., *The Limits of Safety: Organizations, Accidents, and Nuclear Weapons*, Princeton: Princeton University Press, 1993.

———, 'Why do States Build Nuclear Weapons? Three Models in Search of a Bomb', *International Security*, vol. 21, no. 3, Winter 1996/7.

Sagan, Scott D. and Jermi Suri, 'The Madman Nuclear Alert: Secrecy, Signaling, and Safety in October 1969', *International Security*, vol. 27, no. 4, Spring 2003.

Sardesai, D.R. and Raju G.C. Thomas, eds., *Nuclear India in the Twenty-First Century*, New York: Palgrave-Macmillan, 2002.

Shahandeh, Behzad. 'Confidence Building Measures in the Persian Gulf', *Discourse: Iranian Quarterly*, vol. 2, no. 2, Fall 2000.

Sheppard, Ben, 'US Missile Defence Plans Consign ABM Treaty to History, but Where do the Allies Go from Here?', *Jane's Information Group*, 3 May 2001.

Singh, Jasjit, 'Arms Race in the Region: Myths and Reality', *Strategic Analysis*, vol. XVIII, no. 5, Aug. 1995.

———, 'Pakistan's Future War', *Strategic Analysis*, Aug. 1999.

———, ed., *Asia's New Dawn: The Challenges to Peace and Security*, New Delhi: Knowledge World, 2000.

Sidhu, W.P.S., Brian Cloughley, John H. Hawes, and Toresita G. Schaffer, *Nuclear Risk-Reduction Measures in South Asia*, Report no. 26, Washington, D.C.: Henry L. Stimson Center, Nov. 1998.

Sloan, Elinor, 'Beyond Primacy: American Grand Strategy in the Post-September 11 Era', *International Journal*, vol. LVIII, no. 2, Spring 2003.

Sokov, Nikolai, 'Russia's Approach to Nuclear Weapons', *The Washington Quarterly*, vol. 20, no. 3, Summer 1997.

Srivastava, Anupam and Seema Gahlaut, 'Curbing Proliferation from Emerging Suppliers: Export Controls in India and Pakistan', *Arms Control Today*, Sep. 2003.

Stern, Jessica, *The Ultimate Terrorists*, London: Harvard University Press, 2000.

Synott, Hilary, *The Causes and Consequences of South Asia's Nuclear Tests*, Adelphi Paper 332, London: Oxford University Press, Dec. 1999.

Talbott, Strobe, 'Dealing with the Bomb in South Asia', *Foreign Affairs*, Mar./Apr. 1999.

Tellis, Ashley J., *Stability in South Asia*, Rand Report, US: Arroyocenter, 1997.

———, *India's Emerging Nuclear Posture: Between Recessed Deterrent and Ready Arsenal*, US: Rand, 2001.

UN Institute for Disarmament Research, 'Nuclear Terrorism', *Disarmament Forum*, no. 2, Geneva: UN Institute for Disarmament Research, 2003.

Waldman, Amy, 'India Announces Steps in Effort to End its Conflict with Pakistan', *The New York Times*, 3 May 2003.

Waltz, Kenneth N., *The Spread of Nuclear Weapons: More May be Better*, Adelphi Paper no. 171, London: International Institute for Strategic Studies, 1981.

Wiseman, Geoffrey, *Concepts of Non-Provocative Defense: Ideas and Practices in International Security*, New York: Palgrave, 2002.

Wolfsthal, John B., 'Asia's Nuclear Dominos?', *Current History*, vol. 102, no. 663, Apr. 2003.

Yuan, Jing-Dong, 'Chinese Responses to U.S. Missile Defenses: Implications for Arms Control and Regional Security', *The Nonproliferation Review*, Spring 2003.

Zuberi, Matin, 'Nuclear Oceans', *Journal of Indian Ocean Studies*, vol. 10, no. 1, Apr. 2002.

RCSS PUBLICATIONS

- *Defence, Technology and Cooperative Security in South Asia: Report on the Proceedings of the Tenth Summer Workshop* (RCSS, 2004)
- *Terrorism in South Asia: Impact on Development and Democratic Process* (SIPRA, 2003)
- *South Asia and the War on Terrorism* (India Research Press, 2003)
- *Shaping the Future–A South Asian Civil Society Dialogue* (RCSS, July 2002)
- *Small Arms and Human Insecurity* (RCSS, July 2002)
- *SAARC in the Twenty-First Century: Towards a Cooperative Future* (July 2002)
- *Memories of a Genocidal Partition: The Haunting Tale of Victims, Witnesses and Perpetrators* (RCSS, July 2002)
- *South Asian Security: Futures*
  A Dialogue of Director's Regional Strategic Studies Institutes (March 2002)
- *Security and Governance in South Asia* (September 2001)
- *Globalization and Non-Traditional Security in South Asia* (September 2001)
- *Security in the New Millennium* (India Research Press 2001)
- *The Simla Agreement 1972—Its Wasted Promise* (Manohar 2001)
- *Security Studies in South Asia: Change and Challenges* (Manohar 2000)
- *People-to-People Contact in South Asia* (Manohar 2000)
- *South Asia at Gun Point: Small Arms and Light Weapons Proliferation* (RCSS 2000)
- *CBMs in South Asia: Potential and Possibilities* (RCSS 2000)
- *Confidence Building Measures in South Asia* (RCSS 1999)
- *Ethnicity and Constitutional Reform in South Asia* (Manohar 1998)
- *Regional Economic Trends and South Asian Security* (Manohar 1997)
- *Diplomacy and Domestic Politics in South Asia* (Konark 1996)
- *Nuclear Non-proliferation in India and Pakistan: South Asian Perspectives* (Manohar 1996)
- *Refugees and Regional Security in South Asia* (Konark 1996).

RCSS Newsletter

A quarterly bulletin, it publishes a brief report of RCSS activities, presentations at its workshops on topics of contemporary interest and news and programmes of the RCSS and its alumnae.

RCSS Policy Studies

27 Nepal's Maoist Movement and Implications for India and China (forthcoming)

26 Elite Perceptions in Foreign Policy: Role of Print Media in Influencing India-Pakistan Relations, 1989-1999 (forthcoming)

24 River Water Sharing Problem Between India and Pakistan: Case Study of the Indus Basin Water Treaty (forthcoming)

23 Christianity and Political Conflict in India: The Case of Gujarat (June 2002)

22 Nature and Dynamics of Conflicts Over Privatization of Potable Water (June 2002)

21 Governance and Defence Spending: View from South Asia (August 2001)

20 Globalisation and the Multinational Corporations (MNCs) in South Asia (July 2001)

Fellowship in South Asian Alternatives (FISAA) Monograph

- Water, Power And People: A South Asian Manifesto on the Politics and Knowledge of Water (1997)
- The Nuclear Debate: Ironies and Immoralities (1998)

Others

- *Directory of Individuals and Institutions Engaged in South Asian Strategic Studies* (1998).